W9-AQQ-465

Trees

THE BALANCE OF LIFE
THE BEAUTY OF NATURE

Trees
Pierre Lieutaghi

Distributed in the USA and Canada by
Sterling Publishing Co., Inc.
387 Park Avenue South
New York, NY 10016-8810

First published in the UK and USA in 2011 by
Duncan Baird Publishers Ltd
Sixth Floor, Castle House
75–76 Wells Street
London W1T 3QH

Conceived, created and designed by Olo éditions
www.oloeditions.com

Copyright © Olo éditions 2009
Copyright in the English-language edition
   © Duncan Baird Publishers 2011
For copyright of photographs see page 192 which is
to be regarded as an extension of this copyright

Translated by Rosemary Rodwell in association with
First Edition Translations Ltd, Cambridge, UK

All rights reserved. No part of this book may be
reproduced in any form or by any electronic or
mechanical means, including information storage and
retrieval systems, without permission in writing from
the publisher, except by a reviewer who may quote
brief passages in a review.

Credits at Duncan Baird Publishers
Managing Editor: Christopher Westhorp
Managing Designer: Suzanne Tuhrim

Created by Olo éditions
Editorial and Design: Nicolas Marçais and
   Philippe Marchand
Scientific Consultant: Marc Rumelhart

Library of Congress Cataloging-in-Publication Data

Lieutaghi, Pierre.
 Trees : the balance of life, the beauty of nature /
Pierre Lieutaghi. -- 1st ed.
   p. cm.
 Includes bibliographical references and index.
 ISBN 978-1-84483-927-8 (alk. paper)
1. Trees. 2. Trees--Ecology. 3. Trees--Pictorial
works. I. Title.
 QK475.L56 2011
 582.16--dc22

                         2010042925

ISBN: 978-1-84483-927-8

10 9 8 7 6 5 4 3 2 1

Typeset in Gravur Condensed and Andrew Samuels
Color reproduction by Colourscan, Singapore
Printed in China by Imago

For information about custom editions, special sales,
premium and corporate purchases, please contact
Sterling Special Sales Department at 800-805-5489
or specialsales@sterlingpub.com.

Notes:
Measurements are given in metric form followed
by the nearest imperial equivalents, rounded up
or down accordingly, in brackets.

PIERRE LIEUTAGHI

Trees

THE BALANCE OF LIFE
THE BEAUTY OF NATURE

DUNCAN BAIRD PUBLISHERS

LONDON

Despite being highly visible and potentially useful, the tree remained an "outsider" in Western cultures for a long time. Although the tree has, naturally, always had a place in rural environments, it was introduced into towns at a relatively late stage. Only people such as hunters, woodcutters and charcoal-burners penetrated the world's wild, remote forests – and even then they feared an encounter with bears or wolves, or perhaps witches and goblins. Modern city-dwellers may still be reluctant to venture into such untamed places alone.

In the nineteenth century, landscape painters began to perceive trees as aesthetically pleasing elements to be included in their pictures. Later, the Impressionists, whose works often recreate the play of light in trees, were influential in further shaping modern feelings about nature. But it was not until the twentieth century that trees came to be valued as living organisms in their own right, worthy of attention and respect – above all for their long lifespans, which often stretch back beyond the boundaries of human memory. Only the unwise ignore the powerful relationship between trees and time.

Not only is the tree much older, but it is also much taller than any other living creation – it stands out, thrusting up from beneath the ground to meet the daylight. By emerging from concealed depths and reaching into the sky, the tree symbolically bridges a void between the extremes that characterize so much of human experience, wherein hope contrasts with the prospect of death, and abundance is countered by nothingness. The image of the tree intercedes between these polar opposites and helps to encourage a calmer, more accepting attitude toward life's contradictions.

In many of the world's mythologies, assorted forms of life, including human beings, were born from trees, and through the concept of the World Tree the cosmos itself was envisaged as a tree. Irrespective of this imagined past, modern science acknowledges that the destiny of trees will play a crucial role in the future of our biosphere.

In our own day, the stages of forest expansion are well known. On any soil with favourable climatic conditions, if there is no human intervention to stop their growth, trees will proliferate to create permanent forest – indeed, this is the ultimate end of plant life. From the Siberian taiga, with its dispersed woodland containing a limited variety of species, to the Mediterranean forests, whose evergreens are perfectly adapted to dry summers, to the great equatorial rainforests, where there are sometimes more than several hundred tree species per hectare, plant life on Earth ideally evolves to become forest.

Marked by the millions of years which have shaped their diversity and directed floral trends, forests adapt to climates and soils, becoming ever more complex the nearer they are to the equator, where plant life is permanently or near-permanently active throughout the year. Tree cover, once it is well established over centuries, evolves in accordance with the life cycles of the dominant species: a thousand years for the temperate rainforest of great conifers of the American northwest; probably around 500 years for the broad-leaved trees of central Europe – the latter having been too much changed by human activity for any pristine examples still to exist.

Plant respiration was first demonstrated in the late eighteenth century, and by the early nineteenth century the role of forests in protecting soils and regulating water systems was well established (indeed, it had already been alluded to by Plato). Springs do not originate from roots, as was previously thought, but extensive and mature forests do have a definite influence on rain and water circulation. And it is well known that trees absorb carbon dioxide, thereby playing a part in offsetting the damaging release of the same gas through human activity.

Environmental problems have finally become evident to all. But however aware we have become of the ecological role of forests, and however much attention we focus on individual "outstanding" trees (unfortunately, we think less about planting young trees, which would help to safeguard our future), most of us in modern Western society have little contact with wooded environments. Destructive forces exerted by our market-led economy mean that it is less expensive to buy a window made of wood from the tropics than it is to have one produced using oak or ash sourced sustainably from our own forests.

Tree cover is declining dramatically in tropical regions. In response, the growth of "agroforestry" – where the same land is used for both agricultural production and forestry – has brought social and ecological benefits. Economies with temperate broad-leaved forests, including those in Europe, should draw inspiration from this practice and try to manage the forest "from within", as a living environment, and not "from outside", like an abstract "green lung" that is supposed to get along on its own. From being an obedient "outsider", there to be ruthlessly exploited, the tree has at last acquired the status of a partner whose own needs have to be taken into account. The future of forests will not be played out at a distance – it requires a commitment from the whole of humanity.

There are many books that go into detail about the life of trees and forests. In contrast, this book focuses the power and beauty of trees, with stunning photographs accompanied by short textual accounts that explain or comment on the image. Both elements aim to highlight the unique character of trees in all their amazing variety, as well as to evoke wonder and to encourage readers to reflect on the urgency of conservation, thereby making us think again about how we use nature.

Trees, these sturdy supporters of life, represent a world that remains distant to many of us and yet is more essential than it has ever been to our well-being. That the paper on which these words and images have been reproduced is derived from woodpulp serves as a fitting celebration of the fundamental role that the tree has played from the beginning in the magnificent and dangerous adventure of humankind.

Pierre Lieutaghi

Contents

green

jewels

green jewels (1)

The tree's embryo, like that of any plant, contains a development plan that will enable it to thrive both under the earth and in the air, by growing and branching out. Its growth upward is ensured by cells concentrated in its buds and at the ends of the roots, and its capacity for growing branches is indefinite, which means that this process continues for the whole of the tree's life.

But what has enabled the tree to grow taller than all other plants is the accumulation system that is responsible for its increase in thickness: wood. With wood, the tree not only has a skeleton, it also has the living network of a giant energy factory. There are xylem pipes, which bring up water and minerals from the roots; phloem tubes, which send back liquid

green jewels (1)

organic nutrients – food – from the leaves; and a pump, which circulates these saps.

The tree's trunk expands outward. Toward its edge, beneath the bark, the tree thickens by means of a thin layer of cells, growing to add a ring of wood each year (true of trees in temperate regions with definite seasons). The tree's "load-bearing capacity" comes from its trunk, the diameter of which keeps pace with the expansion of the tree-top (crown) and the roots.

In its magnificent programming, the tree seems to replicate itself endlessly. When a branch appears it is really nothing more than a tree growing on a tree – a new youngster grafted into the parent, the original reproducing itself and restoring youth to the whole. . .

anatomy of the tree

///

The tree is made up of three distinct but continuous parts, each of which plays a particular role in maintaining the tree's life and its exchanges with its environment: its roots anchor it in the earth, its trunk is a conduit between the earth and the sky, and its top – the branches, leaves, flowers and fruits – opens out to the air above. The tree takes a variety of forms and grows to a greater or lesser degree depending on its species, the climate and the nature of the soil it is in. A tree is distinguished from other plants by its volume, foliage, density and height (generally, only individuals above 5–7m/16–25ft when fully grown are considered to be trees).

The first tree life appeared on Earth about 370 million years ago. These tree ferns – a genus called *Archaeopteris* – reached 20–30m (65–100ft) in height. When the ferns spread in the form of forests, the oxygen they released transformed the atmosphere, favouring the development of animal life. Then came conifers, at the beginning of the Secondary (or Mesozoic) Era, approximately 230 million years ago, followed by hardwoods.

Trees are like green jewels encrusted in the soil, providing both traces of the past and apparently everlasting forms of life with impressive records of growth and longevity, going far beyond those of the animal kingdom.

///

The famous "amorous baobabs" of Morondava, Madagascar, demonstrate their extraordinary clinch and are reputed to bring good luck to any couples who come to embrace beneath them. There are eight species of baobab in the world, six of which are native to Madagascar.

TREES COMMUNICATE WITH EACH OTHER. WHEN PLACED UNDER ATTACK (BE IT FROM VORACIOUS WILDEBEESTS OR AN INVASION OF CATERPILLARS), TREES SECRETE ETHYLENE, WHICH INCREASES THEIR PRODUCTION OF TANNINS AND MAKES THEIR LEAVES INEDIBLE. CARRIED ON THE WIND, THIS GASEOUS SUBSTANCE ACTS AS A WARNING TO NEIGHBOURING TREES, PRODUCING THE SAME CHEMICAL REACTION IN THEM EVEN BEFORE THEY EXPERIENCE THE DANGER FIRST HAND.

roots that nourish

The roots anchor and maintain the life of the tree, ensuring its stability and providing it with mineral salts and water. The tree takes up these resources through the gigantic pump formed by its xylem pipes, phloem tubes and network of roots: from root hairs to rootlets and from secondary roots to main ones, the roots use their fine membranes to absorb the slightest moisture from the soil, which is pumped up the trunk toward the branches and leaves. The roots of most trees are made up of a mass similar to that of the branches, but arranged differently. According to popular belief, roots penetrate deep into the earth because they are seeking to escape light and are attracted by water. But although the roots of some trees can go down as far as three times the height of the tree they are supporting, others – like those of the amazing fig trees (left) of Norfolk Island in the Pacific Ocean – start with a "high collar" of long draperies which spread out majestically above the ground.

trunks and branches

Perfectly vertical and sturdy, the trunk's primary role is to support the upper parts of the tree. The sapwood, lying between the centre and the bark, acquires a new ring of wood each year while the bark thickens, gradually adding to the trunk's circumference (wood can be dated by looking at growth rings). The trunk is connected to the roots at its collar and ceases to be a trunk at the level where the biggest branches grow. The aerial parts of the tree (left), from large branches to secondary and smaller branches, spread out freely in space, offering their foliage to the sun, wind and rain. While some trees soar vertically, in a bid to tower above their surroundings, there are others that extend horizontally. The eucalyptus trees on Phillip Island in Australia (following pages) establish their foliage about 10m (33ft) from the ground and their branches seem very respectful of one another (this phenomenon – where gaps are left between treetops – is known to tropical botanists as "crown shyness").

bark

The bark is comparable to the skin of the tree, and over time – and according to the species – it assumes different forms and textures: smooth, ridged, lumpy, gnarled or peeling. Protecting the tree from the elements, extremes of temperature and disease, bark varies in density and its thickness increases with age. A sort of dead tissue covers the xylem and phloem tubes through which the life-giving saps circulate. The bark may be white, grey, yellow, green, red, brown, black or mottled; it is impermeable to

water yet at the same time it is pierced with millions of tiny pores through which oxygen from the air can reach the living cells of the tree. Whether it is the plane tree, the Tasmanian gum tree, the sweet birch (opposite at top right, bottom left and bottom right, respectively) or the eucalyptus (above and opposite, top left), the colour palette of barks is a delight to the eye.

leaves

The miracle of leaves (above, the distinctive foliage of a Japanese maple) lies in photosynthesis. Leaves owe their green colour to chlorophyll, the plant equivalent of our haemoglobin. Under the effect of light, the grains of chlorophyll contained in leaves capture the carbon dioxide in the air and extract the carbon from it. Combined with water from the soil, this then turns into glucose, while the oxygen is released back into the atmosphere. In doing this, these tiny power stations transform the crude sap that

rises from the roots to the leaves into elaborated sap, which is essential for the tree's growth, at the same time as returning fresh air to the environment. In autumn, because there is less sun, the chlorophyll in deciduous trees disappears, which makes the leaves change colour; deprived of food, the leaves then dry up, fall to the ground and die.

flowers and fruits

Flowers are the tree's sexual organs, responsible for the tree's reproduction. They suddenly blossom on branches and are often arranged in groupings known as inflorescences. Performance is crucial. The passive tree needs foreign carriers (insects or the wind) in order for the male genes (contained in the grains of pollen) and the female genes to meet. The journey may be long or short, depending on whether the stamen (the male organ) and the pistil (the female organ) are to be found in flowers of different trees, of the same tree or even in the same flower (if the tree is hermaphrodite). All being well, the pistil grows, ripens and is transformed into fruit, which itself contains seeds – fertilized eggs which are then dispersed by animals (on their fur or in their faeces), the wind or water. The flowers on these apple trees (left) are bursting with life and with the promise of delights to come.

a living being

///

Just like a human being, a tree is born, lives and dies. Like a human it breathes, eats, grows and reproduces. Its roots fix it in the ground, enabling it to draw up water and various minerals and store nutrients. The water and nutrients circulate toward the edge of the trunk beneath the bark, and the trunk itself propels the branches as high as necessary to reach the light. A tree's leaves capture not only the heat of the sunlight, carbon dioxide and moisture from the air, but also various minerals such as phosphorus, potassium, magnesium and iron. Nitrogen, too, is supplied – by the decomposition of organic matter in the upper layers of the soil. Surprisingly, 90 percent of a tree's nutritional needs come from the air and only 10 percent from the earth. The rhythm and intensity of a tree's growth depend on the species, its age and the quality of the soil in which it grows, as well as on climatic and environmental conditions. The same tree will shoot upward when situated in a dense forest, but develop outward, increasing as much in girth as in height, when growing isolated in the middle of a meadow. It is also important to note that fast-growing trees have, on average, a shorter lifespan than those that grow slowly.

///

Soft, green and downy, buds (left) on a chestnut tree burst open in the spring air, signalling the end of winter dormancy. These will become the year's new shoots.

IN PREPARATION FOR THE TREE'S PERIOD OF REST, BUDS FORM AT THE ENDS OF THE BARE BRANCHES. ROUND OR POINTED, SMOOTH OR FLESHY TO GREATER OR LESSER DEGREES, THE BUDS ARE OFTEN SLIGHTLY STICKY. THEY SWELL AND BURST IN THE SPRING SUNSHINE, THEN A NEW STEM, A MINIATURE LEAF, SOMETIMES A TINY FLOWERHEAD THAT WAS FORMED THE PREVIOUS SUMMER, UNFURLS AND GROWS – AN APPEARANCE THAT HERALDS THE BEGINNING OF A FRESH LIFE CYCLE.

growth

Higher and higher. . . Few living organisms continue to grow throughout their lives. Trees, of course, grow at different speeds depending on whether they are young saplings, adults or venerable old trees – but as long as their leaves absorb light and their roots pump water, trees grow tirelessly. It is tempting to attribute such prodigious growth to the trunk, whose concentric rings reveal the existence of segments that fit together and enable the tree to lengthen in the manner of a giant telescopic mast. Although this idea is beguiling, it is totally mistaken: a tree always grows through its extremities – the branches and roots – rather than through its trunk. In temperate regions any growth in height occurs mainly in springtime and the trunk's diameter increases in summer, whereas in tropical regions the tree develops throughout the year. These evergreen sequoias (left) in North America seem to touch the sky, providing impressive examples of tree growth.

reproduction

A flying insect drunk on
spring sap (left) and covered
in pollen is lending a hand in
the tree's sexual reproduction.
Dissemination of the fertilized
eggs will take place later,
between spring and autumn
depending on the species,
and each seed that matures
contains the rudiments of
the roots, stem and leaves.
But there is another means
of reproduction, called
"vegetative", which is similar
to cloning: on contact with
the soil, the lower branches
of certain trees develop
roots and give birth to a new
individual, a layer, which has
a potential identical to that of
the original tree. Sometimes a
bud on a shallow root bursts,
forming a sucker that takes
advantage of the tree's food
to grow rapidly; poplars are
known for this. And when
some trauma (inflicted, for
example, by a lightning strike
or a chainsaw) puts an end to
a tree's life, then young shoots
may appear in clumps at the
base of the mutilated trunk.
Most broad-leaved trees – but
notably the chestnut, lime
and hornbeam – have this
capacity for resurrection.

longevity

Trees are some of the Earth's longest-lived inhabitants, none more so than the African baobab, which can survive for as long as 5,000 years. In temperate regions, pines hold the records for longevity. This Great Basin Bristlecone pine (left) with its spiked cones has been established for 4,700 years at an altitude of 3,000m (9,850ft) in eastern California and is nicknamed "Methuselah". Its prize may have recently been stolen by a spruce in Sweden. However, this is not clear – because although the dendrochronological analysis of the underlying wood proves that the root is 9,550 years old, some specialists believe the tree is more likely to be a younger clone from a now-dead mother tree.

the end of life
Trees rarely die of old age – instead, disease, insects and parasites, bad weather and natural catastrophes are all major causes of death. Although we are dependent on trees as much for the air we breathe as for furniture or the fuel for a comforting open fire, humans also endanger trees by overexploiting the planet's forests. Urban trees may fall victim to manmade pollution but entire forests can also perish through natural causes. These sun-scorched camel thorn trees

(*Acacia erioloba*) in the Namib Desert (above) look like fossils. Some 900 years ago this once-flourishing site was fed by a river, but then the climate dried up and dunes cut off the river. The prolonged drought slowly killed off the trees and the climate became too dry for the trees to decompose, leaving this monument to the effects of climate change.

fires

Fires are essential to the natural regeneration process of many forests. Fire helps to dispose of dead leaves and wood, while the resultant ash provides minerals necessary for the growth of vegetation. But many ecosystems suffer from forest fires occurring too frequently, leaving the forest with no time to regenerate. The woodland on the island of Hawaii (left) regularly glows with lava flows when the Kilauea volcano erupts, and these trees will be completely destroyed in a few hours. Forest fires affect the climate of the regions where they occur, leading to peaks in pollution and greenhouse gas emissions, and contributing to deforestation and soil erosion.

In the single year of 2000 some
350 million hectares (865 million acres)
of forest throughout the world
were destroyed by fire.
Eighty percent of this area was
in Sub-Saharan Africa and Australia.

**Each year, 0.3 percent
of the world's forested
area goes up in smoke,
and humans are directly
or indirectly involved in
nearly nine cases out of 10.**

One of the most serious fires in recent times
took place in Australia in February 2009:
more than 3,500 buildings were destroyed.

species

thousands of species (2)

When botany was merely a subordinate branch of medicine and pharmacy, the classifications were somewhat arbitrary and people did not hesitate to link types of plants which are, as classified nowadays, unrelated.

In eighteenth-century Sweden Carl Linnaeus devised a universal system of categorizing organisms, leading to the dividing of things into the taxonomic groupings of kingdom, phylum or division, class, order, family, genus and species – followed, in the case of the plant kingdom, by cultivars and varieties defined by the plant's numbers of pistils and stamens (sexual organs). In his 1753 work *Species Plantarum* (*The Species of Plants*) he applied his system of binomial nomenclature to thousands of plants, and it

thousands of species ②

is still in use today. The first half of the name is the genus, given in Latin (*Prunus, Quercus,* and so on). The second half, also in Latin, is the species name to indicate specificity: thus, the weeping form of the genus willow, or *Salix,* was given the species name *babylonica* by Linnaeus in reference to the weeping Jews exiled in Mesopotamia, who came to pray beneath it. Seed-producing plants are divided into gymnosperms and angiosperms. The seeds of gymnosperms (from the Greek for "naked seeds") form outside the ovule, such as occurs with the *Cycadaceae* and *Coniferae.* The seeds of angiosperms ("receptacle seeds") form within the ovule or fruit – a large classification arranged into eight groups, which include the *Monocotyledonae* and *Eudicotyledonae.* Most broad-leaved trees are angiosperms.

conifers
///

Conifers, literally "cone carriers", appeared on Earth 200 million years ago. They belong to the category of gymnosperms, plants with "naked" seeds, and in the case of conifers these nestle inside the cones, which open at the moment of pollination and dissemination. The foliage of conifers is usually persistent and composed either of needles or minuscule scales arranged in branches. They have very low transpiration rates compared with broad-leaved trees, which enables them to survive in cold climates and arid soils, and they secrete a sticky, antiseptic, healing substance known as resin.

The araucaria (monkey puzzle tree), cedar, cypress, spruce, juniper, yew, larch, pine, fir, sequoia and thuya all belong to the order of conifers or resinous trees, which contains more than 600 species divided into seven families. Conifers adapt to temperate, tropical or subtropical, and especially circumpolar, climates. Thus the boreal forest, or taiga, forms a green ring that is more than 16 million sq km (6 million sq miles) in area, interrupted only by the Bering Strait and the Atlantic Ocean. Mainly composed of frost-resistant pines and spruce, the taiga is the largest forest in the world and makes a magnificent complement to the coloured lightshow of the aurora borealis (following pages).

///
Their crowns are in the sun throughout the year, their feet are protected by a thick carpet of needles and their branches bend without breaking: whether wild or cultivated, fir trees are extremely resistant.

CELEBRATED IN THE GERMAN CAROL "TANNENBAUM", THE CHRISTMAS TREE IS ACTUALLY NORMALLY A SPRUCE OR NORDMAN FIR. CANADA AND DENMARK ARE THE BIGGEST PRODUCERS OF THE ILL-FATED TREE – DESTINED TO BE UPROOTED BEFORE IT REACHES 10 YEARS OF AGE AND END UP, DECORATED WITH TINSEL AND SILVER BALLS, IN THE CORNERS OF FESTIVE LIVING ROOMS, BEFORE ITS NEEDLES FALL.

pines

The pine, an evergreen with persistent needles grouped in twos, threes or fives, is emblematic of the coniferous habitat. Pine cones, full of seeds, are visible from autumn, when their scales have become brown. The pine family is very numerous with a variety of individual species: Scots, maritime, umbrella, black or red pine, and others that bear the name of their place of origin (Monterey, Himalayan, Corsican, and so on), some giant, some of them dwarf. Pine wood is used for carpentry, in flooring and furniture; for the manufacture of pulp; its sap and buds are ingredients in many cough syrups and pastilles; its resin is turned into glue, rosin, turpentine and varnish; and its persistent green colour brings life to gardens all the year round. Could the pine be man's best friend? Hanging, alone, from a crack in the rock on a peak in the Huangshan mountain range in the Chinese province of Anhui, with its long slim trunk and flat crown, this pine (left) survives majestically in a most exposed position.

sequoias

It is often remarked that in the United States everything is on a gigantic scale – and if the American subfamily *Sequoioideae* is anything to go by the tradition of largeness goes back at least 2,700 years. The world's largest tree is a giant sequoia (*Sequoiadendron*), found only in the Sierra Nevada mountain range. The tree, in what is now Sequoia National Park (above), was baptized "General Sherman" in 1879 by the botanist who discovered it and who had fought under Sherman during the American Civil

War. The measurements are dizzying: 83.8m (275ft) tall and more than 31m (102ft) in circumference at the ground; its trunk volume is estimated to be more than 1,487 cubic metres (52,500 cu ft) – enough to make five billion matchsticks! The tallest tree in the world is a coast redwood (*Sequoia sempervirens*) found in 2006 in the Redwood National Park, which runs along the northern coast of California. Known as "Hyperion" this mighty specimen is a little over 115.6m (379ft) high, taller than the 83m (305ft) Statue of Liberty.

bald cypresses

The cypresses of Louisiana (left) are called "bald" because their deciduous foliage – composed of short, flat and soft, pale-green needles – becomes golden, then bright red in autumn before falling in winter, together with the branch that supported it. Bald cypresses originate from the southeastern United States. These slow-growing conifers live from 300 to 500 years and like to have their feet in water – on marshy terrain or even on land that is flooded for several months of the year, hence their other name of swamp cypresses. Their often swollen base, or buttress, gives them a recognizable appearance, accentuated by their roots which put out long fibrous stumps that project upward. These distinctive and intriguing structures are known as knees and each one can grow up to 1m (3ft) tall. The stumps may supply oxygen and/or help to filter out impurities from the groundwater, but their role remains an enigma. Cypress wood is hard and does not rot, so it is much sought after as a building material.

broad-
leaved trees

///

Broad-leaved trees belong to the category of angiosperms, plants whose seeds are enclosed in ovaries that are part of the flower's pistil. The flowers themselves may be female or hermaphrodite. When pollination occurs, the pollen released by the stamens is deposited on the stigma and then penetrates through the style to the ovary, which contains ovules. After this, the ovules turn into seeds and the fertilized ovary becomes the fruit. The seed then contains an embryonic tree, with the two seed-leaves or cotyledons typical of broad-leaved trees. This differentiates them from grasses and liliaceous plants, which have only one cotyledon.

In temperate climates, broad-leaved trees put out new leafy shoots each spring. A tree is most often recognized by its leaves, which are programmed to assimilate chlorophyll – the leaves are said to be "deciduous" if they die when autumn comes and "persistent" if they live for several years. Generally thin and flat, the leaves may be simple or composite, plain or variegated, and so on. Broad-leaved trees appeared on the planet 100 million years after conifers, but today they are in the majority and have a much greater number of families. Because broad-leaved trees transpire a great deal more than coniferous ones, they have a considerable effect on air humidity and quality.

///

In temperate zones, broad-leaved trees are most often found in mixed forests. Here, the hornbeam and sycamore maple share space with the dominant oak.

COMING INTO LEAF AND SHEDDING LEAVES IS PART OF THE CYCLE OF LIFE FOR A BROAD-LEAVED TREE. THE BARE BRANCHES OF WINTER DISAPPEAR FROM VIEW BENEATH ABUNDANT FOLIAGE IN SUMMER. THE BUDS OF SPRING CONTAIN THE MINIATURE FRAMEWORK OF THAT YEAR'S SHOOTS. AT THIS TIME THE LEAF FORMS AN ABSCISSION LAYER BETWEEN THE PETIOLE AND THE STEM. DERIVING FROM THE LATIN "CUT AWAY", THE ABSCISSION LAYER IS THE POINT AT WHICH THE PLANT CELLS WILL SEPARATE FROM ONE ANOTHER IN AUTUMN, ENABLING THE LEAF TO DETACH ITSELF AND FALL TO THE GROUND WITHOUT HARMING THE TREE.

aspens

The aspen is a poplar, whose flowers form long catkins. The French name for it is *tremble*, which derives from the fact that its leaves tremble and rustle at the slightest draught, because their round, wavy-edged leaf blades are held by a long petiole, flattened vertically. The bark is smooth and milky grey to start with, then becomes pockmarked by small black diamond-shaped cavities, which converge to become crevices. Aspens grow quickly but do not live very long. They are happy on low ground and in

higher-altitude terrain, as long as they have their ration of light. In forests, they tend to be found toward the edge, which they colonize by putting out suckers. At one time the tree was planted in numbers along the sides of roads in Europe (above, in Bavaria) to act as a windbreak, and during the early days of high-rise apartment estates it was used to deliver a humanizing touch, but it is hardly ever used now because its pollen grains are highly allergenic. The aspen's soft wood, with short fibres, is used for matches and paper napkins.

beeches

The beech originated in central Europe. Often associated with the oak, the beech is one of the mainstays of temperate forests and it is relatively indifferent to the nature of the soil. This shade-lover can reach more than 30m (100ft) in height. Its dense foliage forms an imposing domed crown, which filters the light and limits the development of the undergrowth. Whatever the beech species, its fine bark, of an aristocratic grey, remains smooth even when the tree has reached maturity. It grows slowly but can live for 300 years. Squirrels and boars, and even curious humans, appreciate the young leaves (tasting of walnuts), and the autumn beechnuts can be eaten roasted as an ecological accompaniment to pre-dinner drinks. The dwarf beech (seen here, left, in the Verzy Forest in Champagne, France), also known as the twisted or parasol beech, has an amazingly contorted trunk and branches.

maples

The maple family (containing the genus *Acer*) numbers more than 100 species. Lobed, palmate leaves are often common identifiers of maple trees as are the fruits made up of two seeds with a wing on either side (the "helicopters" so loved by children). The sugar maple (*Acer saccharum*), whose crimson colours illuminate the forests of Quebec in autumn (left), is the red leaf that adorns the national flag of Canada; its crude sap is collected at the end of winter and made into a delicious syrup. Elsewhere in the world, many Japanese people walk along riverbanks, through parks and over hills for the simple pleasure of admiring the fleeting beauty of the Japanese maple (*Acer palmatum*) with its purple palmate leaves; this elegant tradition is called *momijigari* (literally "maple hunting").

japanese flowering cherries

There are several hundred varieties of Japanese flowering cherry (*sakura* in Japanese), a small ornamental tree belonging to the genus *Prunus*, which is part of the *Rosaceae* family. From the first fine days of April, its branches, with their reddish-brown bark, become laden with pink or white flowers. The Japanese then celebrate *hanami* ("flower viewing"): the blossoming of these flowers represents springtime, with the return of life in all its beauty – but also this is a phenomenon that is fleeting, and it is the short-lived nature of this glory that is one of the aspects contemplated by those who gather together. The custom of *hanami* dates to the eighth century and appears originally to have been linked to Buddhist symbolism and the warrior caste of Samurai, for whom perfection, detachment and the transience of life went hand in hand. Still today, thousands of people gather in Tokyo each evening to eat, drink and chat under the 1,100 cherry trees in Ueno Park for as long as the blossom lasts.

woodless trees

///

Many plants, tall and slender with leafy crowns and trunks of varying diameter, are in fact special trees. According to botanical classification they are monocotyledons (their seed has only a single cotyledon) whose trunks do not thicken because they do not, strictly speaking, produce "wood". Some of these genera, such as the *Yucca*, *Dracaena* and *Aloe*, have a large trunk called a "stipe", which can grow branches. By contrast, most palm trees have their palms directly implanted on the trunk. Other monocotyledons, such as bamboos, grow like perennial trees: the underground part of their stem, the rhizome, puts out hollow stems above ground, called culms, which are sometimes very large and robust. As for tree ferns, these are very ancient forms of plant life which reproduce not by seeds but by means of spores – their leaves, called "fronds", have the appearance of croziers, which unfold as they expand, and a woody interlacing of roots surrounds and supports their stipe. The greatest concentration of plants in the world is to be found in the Amazon rainforest: a green haven of vegetation with foliage that is usually persistent, the sheer luxuriance and density of which denote an ecosystem of incredible richness.

///

Dracaena draco, with its crown of straight prickly leaves, grows in Spain's Canary Islands. This tree-sized member of the *Dracaena* genus produces a red sap popularly known as dragon's blood, with mythical echoes of dinosaurs. The sap or resin is still used as a varnish, incense, medicine and dye.

A LITTLE MORE THAN 300 MILLION YEARS AGO, FORESTS WERE COMPOSED OF PRE-TREES, FERNS AND HERBACEOUS STEMS, SUCH AS GIANT HORSETAILS, WHOSE MAIN STEMS – WHICH COULD ACHIEVE A HEIGHT OF 30M (100FT) – WERE CREATED BY THE PILING UP OF SCALY MATERIAL. THEN DICOTYLEDONOUS TREES APPEARED AND ADAPTED TO A VARIETY OF ENVIRONMENTS. MEANWHILE RARE SPECIES SUCH AS CYCADS PRESERVED THEIR SPECIFIC FEATURES.

palms

Palms belong to the *Arecaceae* family and there are about 2,700 species. Their appearance is that of majestic feather dusters brushing the sky. A palm's growth takes place through the successive appearance of new leaves from the heart of the plant, and its trunk diameter does not increase with age. Botanically, palms are considered to be closer to grasses and orchids than to oaks. Although palms can be planted in a Mediterranean, or even a mild oceanic or maritime climate, they are found naturally only in

equatorial or subtropical regions. For example, the date palm generally grows in the desert, signalling the presence of an oasis. Palm leaves are either pinnate, with leaflets arranged in two parallel rows, or palmate, that is to say with lobes whose midribs radiate from a single point and are arranged in a fan shape, like the sabal palm (above).

cacti

Cacti are succulent plants with an abundance of prickles, which are common to most of the 3,000 species, all bar one of which are native to the Americas. Despite their hostile appearance, the prickles fulfil essential functions: protecting against herbivores, capturing dew, or propagating seeds caught from the fleeces of animals which rub against them. Most cacti have an atrophied form of leaf, which prevents excessive water loss – a survival strategy for the arid environments in which cacti are found. The saguaro cactus (left) is native to the Sonoran Desert region, near the city of Tucson, Arizona (its blossom is the state wildflower emblem). In the spring, green woodpeckers dig shelters in saguaro cacti to make their nests, which are later abandoned to owls and bats. Some saguaro specimens reach 15m (50ft) in height and can hold up to 3,000l (660gal) of water in their main trunk.

bamboo

Its tubular, segmented structure reminiscent of a human backbone, bamboo has been an inexhaustible source of inspiration for painters in the Far East since ancient times. It is a grass that grows at an incredible speed: in favourable conditions some bamboo species can grow by nearly 90cm (3ft) a day and reach 30m (100ft) in three months – that is to say the height of a 10-storey building. Bamboo remains an important and incredibly versatile resource in China and Japan, being utilized to reinforce concrete, make scaffolding or build suspension bridges; it may also be used to make a flute, a fish net, a tray, a rice bowl or chopsticks to eat with. The young shoots of bamboo, rich in potassium and vitamin A, are a staple of the East Asian diet, and the plant also plays a part in traditional medicine. Carbonized bamboo was employed by Thomas Edison during the development of the long-lasting filament for the incandescent light bulb in the 1880s. Golden bamboo (*Phyllostachys aurea*, left), native to China, is one of more than 1,300 listed species of bamboo.

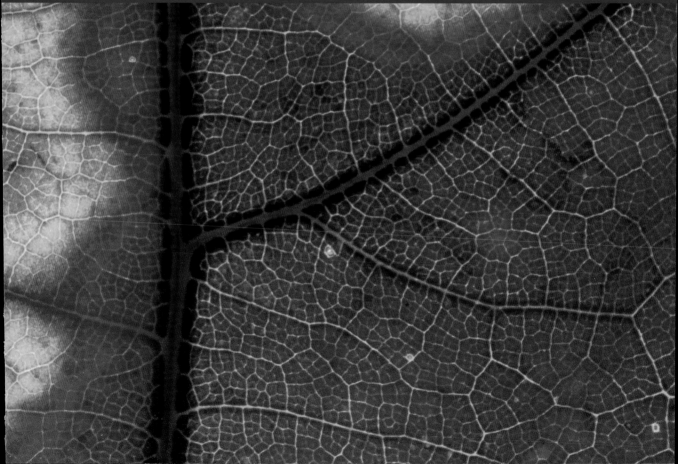

At school children learn that trees purify the air. Later, they are told that trees absorb carbon dioxide and transform it to the advantage of humankind – a particularly valuable attribute because industrialized and overpopulated societies release too much carbon dioxide. Trees thus help to repair the day-to-day damage done to the Earth's atmosphere by manmade pollution and other factors outside human control.

Trees can absorb metals and return them, transformed, to the earth; they can refresh and recycle the air; their roots can aerate and fix soils. But trees, too, can be affected by pollution: their resistance to parasites and insects may become reduced, as may their ability to photosynthesize. Some trees are more robust than others, such as the ginkgo, the venerable

a fragile benefactor ③

tree that survived the radiation from the atomic bomb at Hiroshima. So what are the tree's chances of surviving its battle against pollution?

Unlike animals, trees are not able to run away from dangers, so it is believed that they have evolved diverse protective chemistries instead, although our knowledge of this area is extremely fragmentary. Also, trees are not the only natural organisms capable of carrying out repairs: a healthy bog, a muddy estuary and the like can support vegetation, which has a productivity comparable to that of many forests.

The tree has lasted for millions of years by evolving in symbiosis with its environment, modifying its exchanges with its surroundings as and when necessary. Let's bet that the tree has not yet run out of resources.

trees and
the planet

///

With their incredible diversity of species and amazing ability to adapt, trees contribute to reducing the greenhouse effect: forests in their active phase work ceaselessly to balance the relation between carbon dioxide and oxygen, regulating the climate and moderating extremes of temperature. At the same time, trees are water filters, by means of the continuous cycle of absorption and evapotranspiration, and they also serve as windbreaks and carbon stores. Furthermore, trees contribute generally to the improvement of soils thanks to leaf litter and dead material, which as humus improves the fertility and water retention of the soil when it decomposes. By means of their roots, trees fix the terrain in which they are planted; this, together with the filtration provided by the foliage, reduces erosion. Trees are great managers of the exchanges between earth and sky, and despite being of the utmost importance this resource is under terrible threat: trees are dwindling due to fires, acid rain, storms, avalanches and deforestation linked to the extension of agriculture or the overconsumption of wood. In an attempt to avert disaster, preventative measures have been put in place by various public bodies and organizations, though these remain insufficient. Disregard for the vital functions of trees is due in equal measure to ignorance and indifference, but any laxity of attitude toward their protection contributes to ruining the conditions of life on our planet.

//

The holm oak (*Quercus ilex*) is an evergreen native of the western Mediterranean. It is also known as the holly oak because its leaves resemble those of the holly. For centuries it provided foraging pigs with acorns, which it still does most famously for the Iberian pigs used to produce jamón serrano. Both Pliny and Virgil wrote about this oak, whose leaves were used to produce the first examples of the Roman Republic's *corona civica* (civic crowns).

FORESTS OCCUPY ABOUT 30 PERCENT OF THE EARTH'S LAND AREA, OR APPROXIMATELY 45 MILLION SQ KM (17.4 MILLION SQ MILES) OF APPROXIMATELY 149 MILLION SQ KM (57.5 MILLION SQ MILES). FORESTS ARE NATURAL RESOURCES THAT ARE VITAL TO REDUCING ATMOSPHERIC POLLUTION AND THE GREENHOUSE EFFECT. THOSE WHO MANAGE THEM VARY WIDELY, FROM INDIGENOUS PEOPLES TO INDUSTRIAL CORPORATIONS, AS DO THEIR CONSCIENCES, THEIR INTERESTS AND THE METHODS THEY USE.

a green filter for the atmosphere

Over the course of its growing season – which may be longer or shorter depending on whether it is persistent or deciduous – the tree renews Earth's atmosphere by capturing carbon dioxide, and it refreshes the air due to the moisture it discharges. After being soaked up by the earth, enormous quantities of water are released through transpiration. The volumes of this water, and therefore the amount of humidity generated (which can be measured by a hygrometer), depend on the abundance and persistence of tree foliage. Conifers, especially when densely planted and fully mature, produce thick clouds of mist throughout the year, as seen here covering the Norwegian coastal forest (left). This condensation "traps" certain toxic residues, such as fluorine and lead, which are absorbed and transformed by the trees.

One hectare of trees
produces enough oxygen
for the needs of 40 people.

Half a hectare of trees absorbs 3.1 tonnes of carbon dioxide per year, in other words the amount of carbon dioxide emitted by a car that has travelled 16,000km (10,000 miles).

An adult tree of average height produces
about 120kg (265lb) of oxygen per year.
The carbon represents 20 percent of its weight.

climate

According to the seasons or its internal rhythm, the tree is alternately active and inactive. In cold weather its life slows right down, protected by the scales of its buds and its bark. It confronts the elements without heating or air conditioning, tempering them, holding the snow on its bare branches like winter foliage, acting as a brake to the raging winds and a screen to the cold from the mountains, refreshing and humidifying the air thanks to the evaporation process. If the climate determines the

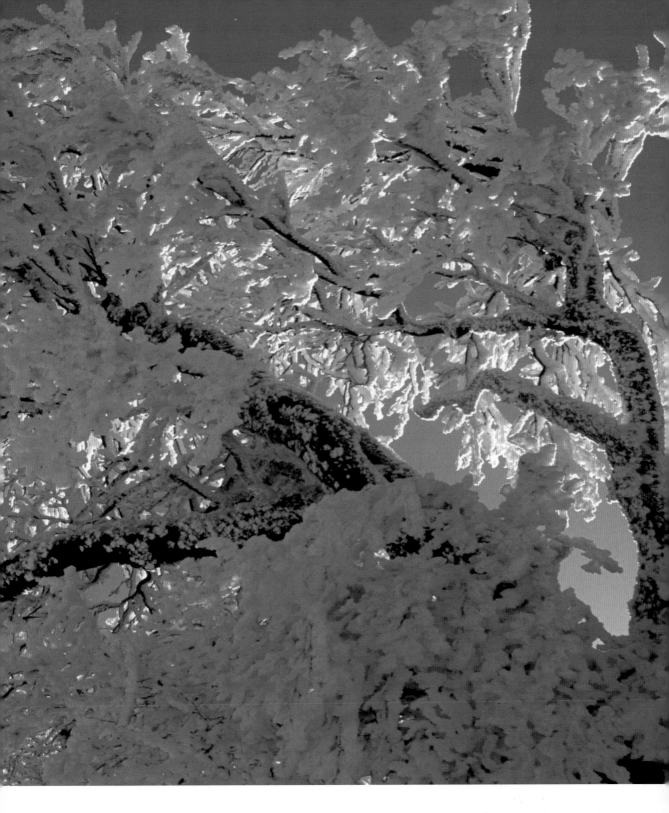

distribution and life of trees, they in return play a part in regulating the climate – locally, regionally and globally. Uproot a large tree next to a house and the cellar will be flooded with water; destroy a forest and the meteorological balance will be disrupted. A tree trunk is a veritable "black box" of information about the climate: with its rings of varying thickness, it can tell us when, in the past, there was a succession of dry years and when there was a great deal of precipitation.

soil improvement

Through its network of roots, the tree has a stabilizing effect on the ground in which it is planted – a precious asset indeed on terrain that is sloping or subject to movement. The tree drains the land, sometimes pumping out excess humidity and facilitating water movement under the surface. The foliage and branches redistribute raindrops and reduce their impact on the ground. Dead leaves (left) form a carpet as they fall, which protects the structure of the underlying soil; and leaf decomposition produces a sort of compost, rich in nutrients. Thus, the ground nourishes the tree and the tree, in its turn, works to regenerate the forest soil. The leaf litter of certain trees, such as the whitebeam, ash, alder and birch, is particularly well known for its beneficial effects in preventing soil deterioration. The timber from these trees remains insufficiently appreciated.

water regulation and purification
In Croatia's Plitvice Lakes National Park, a UNESCO World Heritage Site since 1979, the combination of earth, trees and water creates an ideal green bower. In this scene from the park (above), one can sense the mild temperature, the smells and the rustlings of life. The water seems to be permanently washing the soil and vegetation. Trees help to purify groundwater and they filter the rainwater, capturing its toxic residues and reducing pollution. Having

sufficient trees lessens the likelihood of flooding because the trees will moderate the potentially devastating effects of stormwater by intercepting the rain as well as facilitating the absorption of water into the soil and reducing the volume left over as runoff. Brown bears and wolves continue to frequent this primitive forest, which is mainly composed of beech and pine trees.

trees and
animals

///

Each forest has its animal life, and each tree has its own categories of inhabitants. Although forests are places of relaxation and activity for humans, they are first and foremost natural environments, where all sorts of wild animals cohabit: grizzly bears, elk, caribou and white cranes in the north; tigers, boa constrictors, monkeys and parrots in the tropics; deer, wild boar, foxes, bats, buzzards and raccoons in temperate regions – and these, of course, are just a few of the immense variety of birds, insects and reptiles the forest provides with food and shelter. The humus swarms with worms and beetles; some mammals trample and scratch the forest floor to find larvae and seeds; others eat the accessible fruits and tender leaves and rub their backs against the trunks. The bark is the realm of insects, while the branches support nests, and caterpillars and butterflies feast or lounge on the leaves. Only nimble climbers and birds reach the tree's crown. Each species finds its fill in the forest – even if it means devouring one another, for woodland fauna are mostly carnivorous or omnivorous. But most animals contribute in some way to the forest's regeneration, by degrading organic materials, limiting the number of pests, providing their own rich excrement and transporting seeds and pollen. This life of interdependency is what is meant by an "ecosystem".

///

When the leaves appear in springtime, the red deer stag loses its antlers, which will grow again in the autumn, during the rutting season. After mating with a doe, this symbol of the great broad-leaved forests lives in single-sex packs or alone.

THE ORANGUTAN OF BORNEO AND SUMATRA IS AN ASIAN TREE-DWELLING SPECIES OF GREAT APE (THE NAME MEANS "MAN OF THE FOREST" IN MALAY), WITH IMMENSE ARMS AND PREHENSILE TOES, WHOSE MEMBERS SPEND THEIR WHOLE LIFE IN THE TREE CANOPY, WHERE THEY ARE BORN AND FEED. ONLY THE MALES DESCEND OCCASIONALLY TO THE GROUND. IT IS THOUGHT THAT BORNEO'S ORANGUTANS MAY HAVE DISAPPEARED BY 2020, VICTIMS OF HABITAT DESTRUCTION AS A RESULT OF ILLEGAL LOGGING, THE CONVERSION OF THE ISLAND'S TROPICAL FOREST INTO PALM OIL PLANTATIONS AND FOREST FIRES DESIGNED TO "CLEAN UP" THE SPACE.

up in the treetops

Those small mammals which are capable of scaling trees quickly and leaping among the foliage, on either two legs (monkeys) or four (squirrels), usually have a tail to aid their balance. Tails can also be used to fend off predators, though the Zanzibar Red Colobus monkey (left, in Jozani Forest within the Jozani–Chakwa Bay National Park) has an additional form of deterrent in the form of its strong body odour. This species of red colobus, endemic to Zanzibar, has a black face surrounded by long white hairs; its tail is longer than its body, sometimes reaching more than 80cm (2ft 6in). Its vegetarian diet consists of young shoots, seeds and unripe fruit, and much of the time is spent foraging and eating in groups then resting between meals. Similarly docile once they have finished eating are hunting animals, such as these lions (following pages) in Tanzania's Lake Manyara National Park – often to be found sitting in old acacias to digest their kill in tranquillity.

nests

The forest woodpecker (above, a Black Woodpecker in the forest of the Vosges Mountains, France) has always had an amicable arrangement with trees. The wood of many trees, such as beech, oak and lime, often becomes damaged and decayed during their lives due to infestation by insects or fungi. In a way a woodpecker acts as a tree's dentist, keeping it healthy in exchange for the right to roost inside the trunk. The woodpecker is capable of covering 300ha (740 acres) of forest in its search for insects

and berries, and during these forays it identifies weakspots in trees – the equivalent of dental caries – by drumming on the bark. Excavating the damaged wood creates a cavity in which to nest. As for the Golden or European Oriole (above), it builds a nest at the tops of trees, in a fork or hanging on a branch, using material (twigs, plant fibres, grasses) found on the ground. Although the shelter is sturdy, it is used only from May to August. For the rest of the time, despite its name, the bird prefers to enjoy the warmth of Africa.

the tree as food store

The argan tree is found in southern Morocco and Algeria; it has thorny branches, persistent leaves and can grow to about 10m (33ft) in height. Its fruit is similar to a large olive, but it can have up to three nuts, which contain tiny kernels like almonds. For centuries the Berber peoples have traditionally extracted an oil by roasting the kernels. Argan oil has become much more widely known in recent years, prized as a foodstuff for its richness in vitamins and fatty acids, and as a cosmetic for its ability to nourish and moisturize tired skin. The seeds can be used in cooking, adding an interesting flavour – a little like hazelnuts. Herds cannot graze among the trees from May to August while the fruit ripens, but after that fearless and greedy goats will gobble them straight from the tree, climbing up to the highest branches (left, in Morocco) to eat the shoots and flesh of the fruit. The hard stones pass through the goats and the locals collect them from the droppings.

minifauna   Although the tree is wonderfully equipped for photosynthesis it lives in symbiosis with a near-invisible army of helpers which enable it to extract the mineral salts it needs. This minute population busies itself cutting up leaves and wood into smaller and smaller pieces, burying them in the ground and degrading organic matter into elementary particles, which are then available to the tree. Caterpillars, larvae, dustmites, woodlice and earthworms do the hard work, which is finished off by fungi,

protozoa and bacteria. The Great Capricorn Beetle (above) is a wood-eating species which inhabits old trees, often oaks, and plays its part in the natural management of the forest. The female lays her eggs in the bark; the larvae dig long tunnels through it toward the sapwood. Not only do these tunnels allow the hatched beetles access to the open air, but they also provide an ideal habitat for some of the tree's microscopic mini-helpers.

dead wood

All sorts of animals find shelter in dead trees, such as this Little Owl (*Athene noctua*; left) which has settled in a hollow trunk. For birds, dead wood holds a superb stock of small prey, such as worms and larvae. Wood-eating insects (such as the Great Capricorn Beetle, previous pages) bore tunnels through it, in turn creating the right conditions for other species to thrive, such as invertebrates or fungi, which can find a home in the wood that they will be helping to break down. Generally, it can be said that about 20 percent of forest fauna depend on dead wood, either directly or indirectly. Contemporary forest managers have realized that maintaining a certain proportion of dead wood within the forest perimeter, either standing or in a pile, is beneficial even if the forest is being worked: it means that the food chains between the various players in the environment's "eco-recycling" can be preserved or even improved.

es and h

umans

of trees and humans ④

The goal of all young, healthy trees is to become forest. Through sexual reproduction and suckering, they will multiply and colonize the space in which they grow, pushing its limits outward. Trees thus appear to represent inexhaustible wealth.

Humans began to exploit trees in Neolithic times: from fuel to building and pharmacopoeia to food. In seventeenth-century France, under King Louis XIV's finance minister Jean-Baptiste Colbert, people started to worry about tree stocks becoming exhausted and it was decided to replant to ensure the resource's continued availability. Nowadays, in temperate regions, most of the wood for industry and the pulp for paper comes from managed forests.

Although the forest remains a place for leisure – to walk, gather food, collect wood or even to hunt – this aspect pales in comparison with the profits to be generated by working it, whether as a private owner or an international company. Forestry regulations can be lax in some parts of the world. Who is not aware that an inexpensive, mass-produced garden table in an exotic wood has helped to endanger an ecosystem on the other side of the world? Trees have always shown a great ability to adapt in response to gradual changes in their environment, but we should remember that these adaptations have hitherto taken place over long periods of time. But today more and more people are questioning whether forests can withstand the far more radical and rapacious effects of modern commercial exploitation.

a vital resource

///

When immense tracts of the Earth were covered by forests, the first humans used wood to make fire, and thus to obtain light, scare away predators, cook their food and warm themselves. With the invention of the axe, wood became the material used to make dwellings, then for the means of transport, particularly shipbuilding. The birth of agriculture, in the Neolithic period, brought the first clearing of land for cultivation; but it was the Middle Ages which saw deforestation on a massive scale, to supply the needs of forges, glassworks and saltworks. Wood and charcoal, together with peat, were for a long time the only fuels, before coal and oil, which are themselves fossil fuels produced by the decomposition of ancient forests. Wood is used less often today for heating, but it continues to represent 50 to 70 percent of energy consumption in some of the world's poorer and more rural areas. From the cradle to the grave, people derive benefit from the gifts of nature that come from the tree, without giving them a second thought: from the stairs they climb to the newspaper whose pages they leaf through (note the word "leaf"), sitting in an armchair in front of a roaring fire, sipping a tea. And if they want to draw, or note down an idea, they grab a pencil and a sheet of paper. . . all made from wood.

///

Log-floating (seen here in Malaysia, left) is one of the oldest means of transporting wood from the places of production to those where it is to be used. But when it is suspected of being the result of "mining" the forest, the sight sends shivers down the spine.

ROUGH WOOD FOR PALLETS, CRATES OR MATCHES, MORE FINISHED WOOD FOR PENCILS, KITCHEN UTENSILS AND TOYS, PRECIOUS WOODS FOR LUTE-MAKING AND MARQUETRY, A RICH COLOUR CHART OF SHADES AND TEXTURES FOR FURNITURE. . . "HEARTS OF OAK", "A WOODEN EXPRESSION", "AS THICK AS TWO SHORT PLANKS", "YOU CAN'T SEE THE WOOD FOR THE TREES" – FEW MATERIALS FORM PART OF OUR DAILY LIFE AND LANGUAGE TO THE EXTENT THAT WOOD DOES.

wood

Where do the patterns come from, on floorboards or furniture, by which a particular wood may be identified? When a tree trunk is cut crosswise it shows concentric rings, which represent the successive layers of wood laid down each year. Certain pieces of wood, such as the butcher's block, have their surface cut against the grain, enabling them to resist repeated shocks. It is when the trunk is sawn lengthwise that the subtleties of texture and lines particular to each species appear. Since the circles are more or less regular, individual protuberances become evident, revealing the existence of a branch, a dry period, and so on. As for the colour of the wood, when it does not signal the presence of bacteria or fungi – great colourists both – then it must result from an alchemy between the tree's cells, the soil and the atmosphere.

wooden buildings

For millennia, wood has been the basic material for human housing. As a renewable resource, it remains an essential one for the construction industry, providing the framework for buildings as well as the doors, the window frames and the shutters. In recent years, more and more buildings have been finished with wood, which provides insulation properties as well as a pleasing appearance. There has also been a renewal of interest in ecological housing, which may be quite rustic, and built with logs, or more futuristic, and built with panels that contain modern insulating materials. The vogue for carefully located wood cabins and other similar shelters combines charm with a respect for the environment – and in temperate regions the wood used for these buildings now comes mainly from managed rather than primary forests. The Jean-Marie Tjibaou Cultural Centre (left) in Nouméa, New Caledonia, was built in iroko wood and glass by Renzo Piano between 1995 and 1998 using a vernacular style to evoke traditional huts.

wood for energy

Felled trees are used primarily for fuel. In 2008, world production of wood for heating reached some 2 billion cubic metres (70 billion cu ft). In Europe, waste from sawmills, in the form of offcuts or sawdust or pellets, is often used to provide an efficient communal heating supply. Wood-burning stoves and cookers use small split logs, or, increasingly, wood in pellet form. Whole logs are reserved for traditional fireplaces, where they have pride of place. It should be remembered that the quality of a fire is determined by the species of tree. Conifers heat very rapidly, but they burn quickly. Hardwoods burn more slowly and give out an excellent heat. Beech is ideal, both for its flame and embers but also for the smell it releases, which means it is often used for smoking food. In an open fireplace, chestnut needs to be watched because it spits as it burns, as does spruce, which emits showers of sparks.

food resources

Fruits and seeds (walnuts, hazelnuts, almonds and so on) which early humans on a subsistence diet once picked from local trees are now part of a global trade. The cool or temperate regions are associated with various types of nut (see left, three pecan nuts on a pecan tree), together with fruit such as plums, apples and pears; the tropical regions with mangoes, bananas, coconuts and dates; and those areas between the two with citrus fruit, peaches, apricots and figs. In temperate regions, the variety of "local" fruits has dwindled at the same time as fruit production has become more industrialized, with orchards often stretching as far as the eye can see (walnut trees, following pages). Generally rich in pigments, fibre and vitamins, fruit is not always soft and sweet – the fruits of both the cacao tree and the coffea tree produce bitter drinks, while olives are bitter and are either pressed to extract their oil or fermented, cured and pickled to make them palatable.

a resource for medicine

In ancient Egypt decoctions of willow leaves were a cure for aches and fevers. Today, willow (*salix* in Latin) bark is the source of salicylic acid, which provides the main component of the synthetic acetylsalicylic acid, better known as aspirin. Nearly 2,000 tree species were used in traditional pharmacopoeia, the forerunner of the pharmaceutical industry.

Phytotherapy is the modern-day form of herbal medicine, devoted to study of the use of extracts and essences with natural origins, such as trees. For example, the cinchona tree produces quinine, a specific remedy for malaria; the loquat tree is known for its antibacterial properties; and eucalyptus leaves are used for treating colds, bronchitis and asthma.

The *Ginkgo biloba* (left) is the sole survivor of a family that flourished 200 million years ago in the Far East and was preserved by monks in China who prized it for its beneficial properties: the fan-shaped leaves and the cherries on the female trees stimulate blood circulation, and are used for combating memory loss and senility.

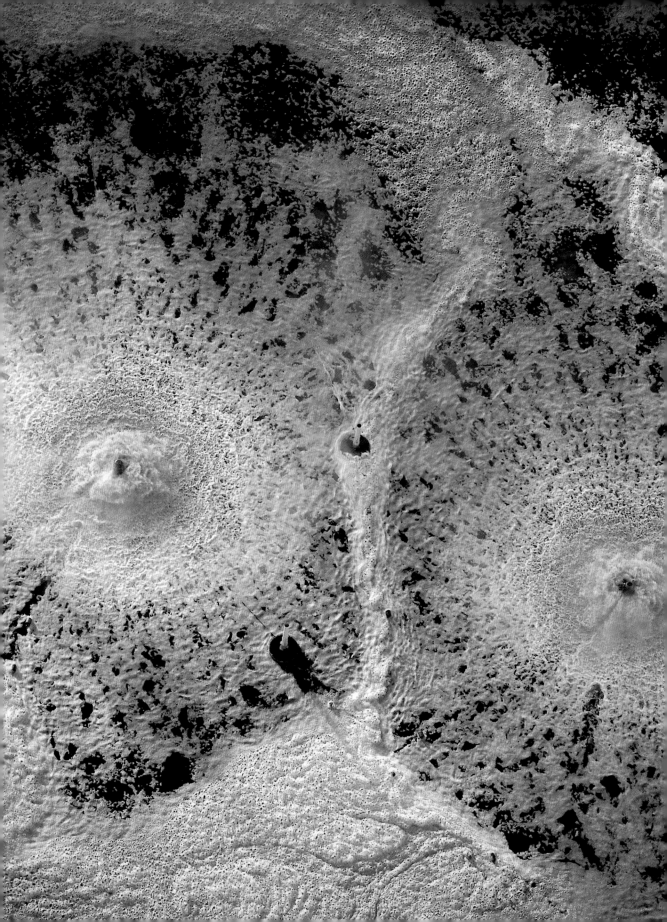

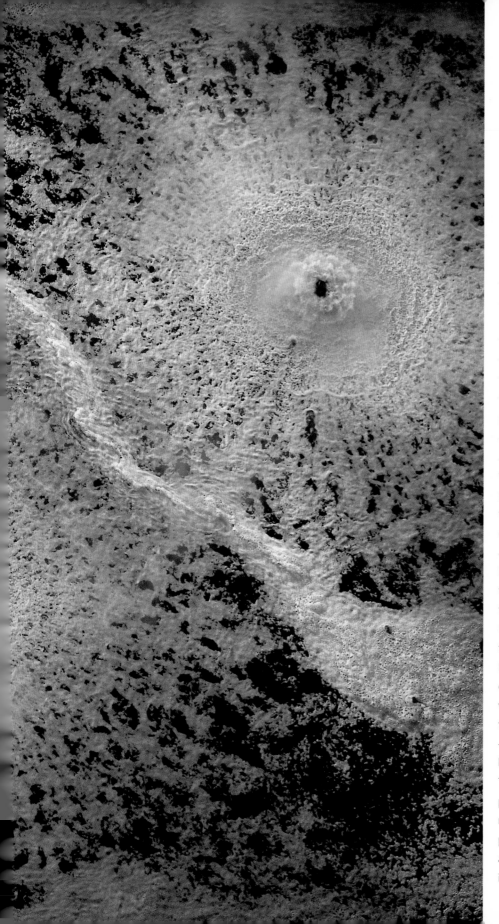

pulp for paper

Invented in second-century China, paper was first produced from a pulp of mulberry or bamboo bark. It reached the West via Persia and Arabia in the seventh century. In Europe, rags were used in its manufacture until woodpulp ushered in the era of industrially produced paper in the nineteenth century. In this process, grinders reduce the wood to shavings then fibres, which are moistened to make pulp; the pulp is then placed on a metal drainer to allow the water to drip off. After this the pulp is passed through cylinders, which press and dry it. In order to make the paper white, chemists have perfected acid baths to eliminate hemicellulose and lignin from the wood fibre, so that only the cellulose is preserved (left, paper pulp is being treated in a Swedish factory). Nowadays, because of environmental concerns, the waste products – which are full of organochlorine residues – are often put through a biological filtration process. To alleviate deforestation, papermakers increasingly recycle – more than 60 percent of all European and American production is now recycled.

natural products
In addition to wood, there are more than 5,000 other natural products that come from the tree: fibres from the raffia palm, tannins and preservatives from the oak and walnut, bottle stoppers (above) and tiles made from the bark of the cork oak, resins, turpentine, essential oils for cosmetics and aromatherapy, and much more. In 1730, near Quito, Ecuador, the French naturalist Charles Marie de la Condamine became the first Westerner to encounter a whitish substance extracted by the

...ndians from a tree (*cahutchu*, or "tear of the tree" in Quechua) belonging to the genus *Hevea*, but better known to us today as the Pará rubber tree. In order to collect this "liqueur" (in Latin, *latex*) from the *Hevea brasiliensis* (above), a spiral cut is made in the trunk and the sap-like extract is siphoned off. The rubber tree is found mainly in the Amazon and in extensive plantations in Southeast Asia. Each year, about 10 million tonnes of natural rubber is manufactured from latex – nearly all of that production (95 percent) is in Asia.

The "wood" sector creates more jobs than the car industry

Arboriculturist – boatbuilder – botanist – builder of wooden houses – cabinetmaker – carpenter – charcoalmaker – clogmaker – cone gatherer – cooper – coppicer – cork manufacturer – floorer – foliage expert – forest engineer – forest machine operator – forest officer – forester – forestry technician – gamekeeper – joiner – landscape architect – landscape soil expert – lath cutter – log merchant – log transporter – logger – long sawyer or head sawyer – lumberjack – lutemaker – marquetry inlayer – nurseryman – panelmaker – paper manufacturer – parquetry worker – pipe turner – pruner – roofer – saw-sharpener – silviculturist – timber merchant – tree surgeon – trunkmaker – woodcutter – wood expert – wood-heating merchant. . .

stimulus to well-being

///

/

alm and perfectly stable,
e man practising his *tai
i chuan* movements
pposite) under the trees
a park has adopted the
sture Needle at Sea
ottom. The sequences
e is going through have
olourful names such
  Repulse the Monkey,
atting the Horse's Neck
d Bird in Oblique Flight.

Many descriptions, such as "lofty", "rooted", "solid", "cool", "bursting out", "fading", "stripped bare" and "reborn" can be applied to both people and trees, an indication of the powerful affinity that humans feel with trees, benign organisms that protect us and promote our peace of mind. Forests are places where we can get back in touch with our inner selves, where we can walk on soft ground, breathe in natural scents, taste berries, listen to the leaves crackling – all the senses are awakened in the subdued light and stress melts away like snow in the sun. The tranquillity can occasionally be disturbed by gunshots, the roar of a chainsaw or the cry of a bird flying off after being unsettled, but otherwise trees have such power to calm that, centuries after having cut them down to use their space, we replant them in towns, along streets and thoroughfares, in schoolyards, parks and gardens. The fact that in urban environments they are generally not grown for their wood or their fruit now has little importance, because the regenerating effect they have on their location and the atmosphere is matched by their beneficial effect on our psyche and nervous system. Some civilizations, which have not been so distanced from nature, go so far as to consider trees works of art. This conviction has gained ground in the developed world and resulted in all sorts of strategies for planting trees for pleasure, either in isolation or with others, in an environment that has been specially designed for them – even miniaturized ones, which must be the supreme refinement.

places of leisure and pleasure
When we enter a forest we experience changes in light and sound: there is the soft contact of moss, grasses and leaves; little branches that crack underfoot; and the smell of humus and seasonal scents – all of which affect our brains in a mysterious way to produce a cascade of reactions, physical, sensual and mental. A Sunday afternoon walk in the forest with the family can be an opportunity to instruct a younger generation in woodland lore,

or perhaps it provides the perfect setting for a picnic and a game of hide and seek. Alone in the forest, you are able to daydream, as you walk or look for mushrooms. Or perhaps you will imagine yourself having a more primal connection with trees, jumping joyfully through them like a squirrel – something made possible by specially designed aerial walks and slides through the tree canopy – or attempting a hands-on experience through the increasingly popular activity of recreational tree climbing.

light and shade

Towns embellished with plane trees, double lines of poplars along Europe's roadsides, thickets of eucalyptus dotted along California's highways, live hedgerows in the countryside, arbours in private gardens and long canopied paths set in grander estates (such as Oak Alley Plantation, Louisiana, left). Whether they form part of a leisurely walk or a main travel thoroughfare, trees both mark out routes in the landscape and provide welcome shade to those who travel along them. In medieval Europe, planting trees became an economic necessity in response to a shortage of wood caused by overzealous forest clearance. The artistic use of perspective during the Renaissance favoured alignments of trees that cleverly showed buildings off to advantage in their natural surroundings. Everything changed with the advent of the motor car – because it could be fatal to leave a road at speed and strike an unforgiving tree trunk, road-widening measures in the interests of safety have been responsible for the loss of many of these motionless roadside spectators.

the lungs of the city

Since the eighteenth century, trees have formed an integral part of towns and cities by offering pleasurable features which invite urban inhabitants to stroll or relax on a bench in the shade. Englishman Sir Ebenezer Howard (1850–1928) described harmonious green utopias in his book *Garden Cities of To-morrow* (1902), which influenced the planning of many "garden cities" and "new towns" worldwide in the twentieth century. Today, the tree is viewed as an essential

element of our cityscapes, standing alongside small houses, tall buildings and skyscrapers. Tree photosynthesis and transpiration make the air in towns breathable. Trees create a shield against pollution and mitigate the overheating of town centres. Central Park (above) is a 340ha (840-acre) green haven opened in 1859 in the heart of Manhattan in New York – with its elms, oaks and cypresses, the park is proof that even the most bustling city is incomplete without trees.

parks and arboretums

A park combines trees and other plant species in a well-organized space, creating an ambience for a variety of leisure uses. An arboretum, with its dense patches or hints of colour, is a place where the plantings have an underlying educational or recreational purpose. In former times, the parks of the Old World were reserved for the highest social classes, but with the advent of industrialization and urban development parks became more inclusive, fulfilling the dual function of being "green lungs" as well as leisure spaces for all town-dwellers, many of whom had migrated from the countryside. Arboretums, by contrast, are "forest developments" (a kind of observatory to monitor the way acclimatized species behave), "collections" (where a large number of species are gathered together), "themed areas" (to show the diversity of a restricted number of species) or "landscaped areas" (where the priority is to create aesthetic surroundings). The oldest public arboretum in North America is the Arnold Arboretum (left), founded in 1872, at Harvard University.

bonsai

The growing of trees in pots is thought to have originated 4,000 years ago in Egypt, with the practical purpose of making it easier to transport them. In Han dynasty (206BCE–220CE) China miniature landscapes were re-created in wide ceramic bowls and they incorporated waterways, standing stones and small-scale trees. In the sixth and seventh centuries this fashion was introduced to Japan by Buddhist monks where it soon acquired the status of a refined art, with its own rules. The ruling elite practised it under the name of *bonsai* ("growing in a small dish"). By meticulously trimming and binding a young tree's branches and roots, its growth is impeded in such a way that idealized miniatures of the chosen style may be obtained. The oldest *bonsai* is a *Pinus parviflora* in Tokyo that dates from 1500. This juniper tree (left) is in the Moyogi style, characterized by a contorted trunk, with branches bending downward to form crowns at a right-angle to the ground.

forests
in danger

///

The belief that forests are in peril is not a new one. However, trees are a renewable asset and modern European states have attempted to systematize their use of forests and initiate reforestation programmes. Silviculture, the scientific cultivation of forests, was developed in the nineteenth century as a rational answer to the need to exploit our forest inheritance, and it provided a clear step forward, at least in temperate regions. Nearly 10 million sq km (4 million sq miles) of managed or artificially created forests are now harvested, mainly to obtain wood for building, and regenerated systematically. Nevertheless, forests worldwide continue to be damaged in order to clear them for agriculture, or to build transport infrastructure, or to exploit certain tree species without regard to their future well-being. Since the 1980s the perils of deforestation and the consequences for the environment have been known to all. Thus, restrictive conditions are attached to the maintenance and redevelopment of forests, including the replanting of cleared spaces and the establishment of alternating cycles through good use of agroforestry. The effort worldwide to impose controls is evidence of the desire and will to preserve one of humanity's most ancient natural resources and, by extension, to protect the ecological balance of the planet.

THE WORLD APPEARS DIVIDED INTO THOSE WHO DESTROY THEIR FORESTS AND THOSE WHO PROTECT THEM, WITH THE CHIEF CULPRITS TO BE FOUND IN UNDERDEVELOPED COUNTRIES. EVERY YEAR, THE HUMID TROPICAL FOREST SHRINKS BY 170,000 SQ KM (66,000 SQ MILES). AND TO COMPOUND THE ECOLOGICAL DISASTER, SEVERAL THOUSAND TREE SPECIES ARE BECOMING EXTINCT.

///

The terrible spectacle of forested terrain ravaged by humankind's greed for wood, which imperils essential resources. In 2006, about 45 million sq km (17.4 million sq miles), or 30 percent, of Earth's land area was covered by forest – each day the gross area of forest lost is about 360 sq km (140 sq miles).

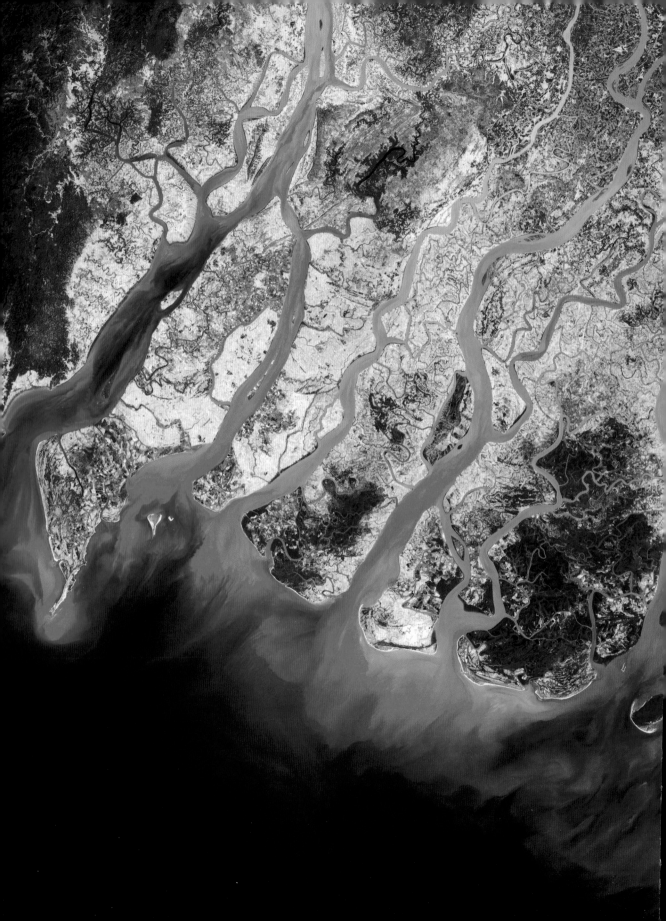

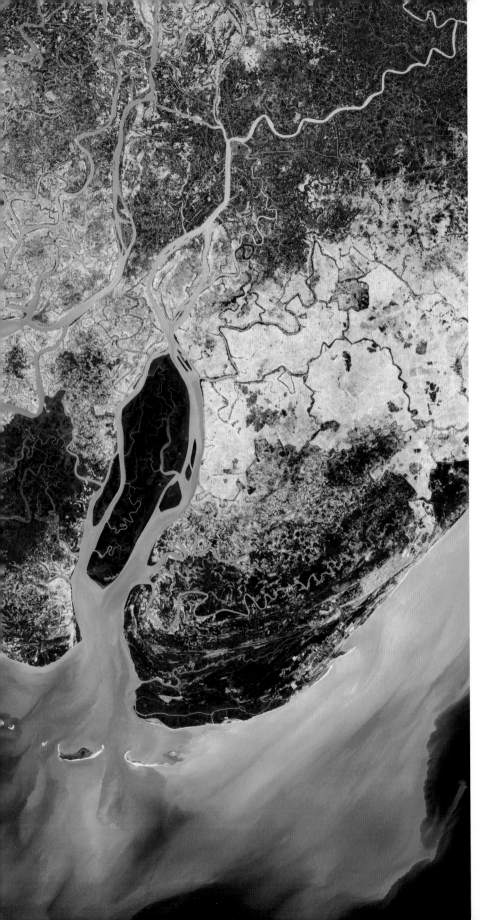

deforestation

Our planet's forests are diminishing. Every day, humans cut down trees and consume wood at a greater rate than the Earth's capacity to replace what has been lost. In the past decade, forests have lost more than 1.3 million sq km (500,000 sq miles) worldwide, which is nearly 3 percent of their total remaining surface area (but about half of that loss has been replanted). Humans have always chopped down trees. The initial clearings were made in order to bring land under agricultural cultivation. Then there was additional felling, to supply the needs of expanding populations and early industrial development. Later, tree loss was intensified by the overconsumption of paper and a desire for exotic woods, often fed by so-called clearfelling of forests. South America, Southeast Asia and Australasia are the regions paying the heaviest price. During the first decade of the new millennium the destruction of mangrove forests, which had provided a protective buffer in the low-lying Irrawaddy Delta of Burma (visible on this satellite image, left), has exacerbated the devastating effects of cyclones and marine erosion.

the amazon

The Amazon rainforest in
South America extends over
approximately 6 million sq km
(2.3 million sq miles) and nine
countries, notably Brazil, which
alone contains 60 percent
of its area. The warm, moist
climate and the vast volumes
of freshwater in the Amazon
River have made this the most
biodiverse region in the world,
with millions of insect species,
1,500 bird species and tens
of thousands of known plant
species – one hectare of
forest may contain hundreds
of species of tree. And, of
course, many indigenous
peoples live there too.

Intensive soybean
cultivation, cattle-rearing,
logging and illegal felling
with scant respect for the
environment could all mean
that the Amazon rainforest
may have lost 260,000 sq km
(100,000 sq miles) or more
of jungle in the past decade.
Scientists are worried about
the effects of this on the
planet's climate. The fate of the
rainforest is largely in the hands
of the Brazilian government
and, encouragingly, there
are signs that the Amazon
Protected Areas Program
(APAP) is helping to slow
down forest loss.

The global annual quantity of wood and paper that is not recycled could heat 50 million homes for 20 years.

Half the surface area of the world's forests has totally disappeared and 80 percent of the remaining space has been seriously degraded.

In the United States, about 50 million newspapers are bought daily, most of which are simply thrown in the bin. If every American recycled 10 percent of their newspapers, it would save the equivalent of 25 million trees per year.

sustainable development

In 1990 the G7 countries proposed an international convention to protect forests. Good intentions always come up against solid obstacles: national sovereignty, scarcity of alternative export-sources for the countries concerned, the strength of world trade (some of which is illegal). In the absence of any regulatory power, the United Nations' Food and Agriculture Organization (FAO) works with states, international organizations and non-governmental organizations (NGOs) to promote sustainable forest management. Each country then legislates measures and a consensus emerges in favour of common criteria. In 2005 nearly 2.5 million sq km (1 million sq miles) of forest was certified to protect it from unsustainable exploitation. The traceability of wood is a useful tool not only for the governments of producer countries but also for the consumers in importing countries. Sustainable forest development is in everyone's interests. Here (left) a nursery of Douglas firs is inspected – the trees are to replant areas ravaged by fire.

e of ins

iration

sources of inspiration ⑤

The transition from a rural world to an urbanized one has transformed the relationship that humans have with trees and forests. What was a daily, physical contact has changed into something abstract and metaphysical. But, curiously, the tree has never ceased to be a living totem, serving as both a symbol and a model of organization – whether describing, interpreting or forecasting, a structure with roots and branching parts is used in many spheres, from genealogy to computing. Do we make these connections just from the outward appearance of the tree, with its branches opening out to embrace space, or is there some more mysterious life principle at work?

The idea that trees are sacred, far from being confined to ancient

sources of inspiration (5)

mythology and "primitive" religions from remote corners of the planet, runs deep in Western culture; within Europe, the forests were once places of worship. Gothic cathedrals provide further evidence of this association, with their tree-like arches and pillars. The protective figure of the ancient tree, motionless and silent, embodies knowledge of the past, while the collective nature of the forest evokes the memory of a lost wholeness. Both individuals and societies need to draw on the resource of trees to get back in touch with their inner selves. The forest is the ideal place to seek to access timeless poetic wisdom, and heavily wooded lands provide the backdrop for countless stories and legends, from the fairytales of the Brothers Grimm to the epics of J.R.R. Tolkien.

sacred trees

///

n the so-called "primitive" religions, where natural phenomena are believed to possess a sacred mystery, trees are often considered to be powerful intermediaries between humans and the supernatural. Spirits are sometimes thought to reside in trees, using the roots and the branches to maintain contact with forces buried in the depths of the earth or flowing through the immense sky. It is not the tree itself that is worshipped, but the power manifested through it. Some tree varieties are linked to a particular divinity: so Greek mythology invested vines, ivy and pines with the attributes of Dionysus, the god of earthly pleasures. Monotheistic religions are more circumspect with regard to trees, though they are often channels of divine will – thus, depending on whether divine will is respected or flouted, the tree brings prosperity or punishment. Founding myths have often been connected with specific trees. In the biblical book of Genesis the apple tree (the genus *Malus*, from the Latin for "bad") is linked to original sin, the first condemnation of humans by God. Judas, once he had carried out his betrayal of Jesus, hanged himself from a small tree, which has remained associated with his infamy ever since and is known as the Judas tree. In the seventh paradise of Islam grows the heavenly tree Tuba, whose branches recite chapters from the Quran – only the greatest mystics are allowed to contemplate it.

/// A burnt tree, or one struck by lightning, evokes the anger of the gods. In many parts of the world people hesitate to cut one down, believing that it might yet revive or that an obscure power continues to live in its charred body.

IN THE ANCIENT WORLD THE GREEKS THOUGHT THAT EVERY TREE, AND PARTICULARLY THE OAK, WAS INHABITED BY A HAMADRYAD, A TYPE OF DRYAD (A FORM OF NYMPH) WHO WAS BONDED TO THE TREE, ENTRUSTED WITH ITS CARE AND WOULD DIE WHEN THE TREE DIED. THUS DRYADS AND THE GODS PUNISHED MORTALS WHO HARMED TREES. THE MARLY COURTYARD AT THE LOUVRE MUSEUM IN PARIS CONTAINS A MARBLE STATUE OF ONE OF THESE OAK NYMPHS.

emblem of the gods

In his *Natural History* Pliny the Elder related a Celtic custom, conducted at the foot of an oak tree, which involved Druids sacrificing two white bulls before one of the Druids climbed up the tree to harvest mistletoe with a golden billhook (although botanists point out that mistletoe does not thrive on oaks). This venerable tree – a symbol of power and longevity – was an emblem of the gods Zeus, Jupiter and Odin. The oak has played a part in the stories of many legendary and historical figures, from Robin Hood, who set up his headquarters at the foot of an oak in Sherwood Forest, to King Charles II of England, who escaped by hiding in an oak following his defeat in the last battle of the English Civil War. Martial associations with the oak are strong: oak leaves have long been an important part of military regalia in Germany and the United States; in France, the samne motif adorns the *képi* of generals. The official march of the Royal Navy in the UK is "Hearts of Oak". The oak's nut – the acorn – is also a popular symbol in human culture, as a sign of patience and slowly developing power.

the original apple tree

In the centre of the garden of Eden, God planted the "tree of life" and the "tree of the knowledge of good and evil". He commanded man: "You may freely eat of every tree of the garden; but of the tree of the knowledge of good and evil you shall not eat, for in the day that you eat of it you shall die" (Genesis 2.16–17). Eve had not yet been created from Adam's rib when this warning was given. The serpent persuaded Eve that she would not die if she ate the prohibited fruit, ". . . for God knows that when you eat of it your eyes will be opened, and you will be like God, knowing good and evil" (Genesis 3.5). When Adam and Eve ate the fruit, their eyes were opened and they saw that they were naked and were ashamed. Outraged that they had defied His command and acquired the capacity for rational judgment, God banished the pair from the earthly paradise to deny them the fruit of the "tree of life", which would bestow eternal life. Thus people became mortal and human existence acquired death. This idea of a sacred tree that confers eternal life occurs in many of the world's mythologies.

rebirth and light

The olive branch became a symbol of peace and prosperity because it was carried in a dove's beak to demonstrate to Noah that the Flood was at an end. Olive trees (left) are long-lived and have been grown around the Mediterranean for millennia, providing food and oil for cooking and light. In ancient Egypt, the technique of extracting oil from olives was attributed to the goddess Isis. Zeus's warrior daughter Athena gave her name to the present capital of Greece after growing the hardy tree there. Victors at the games held at Olympia, their bodies glistening with olive oil, wore crowns woven from the tree's branches. The oil was considered sacred and is still used for anointing in some Jewish and Christian sacraments, such as baptism and the blessing of the dying. The olive tree is mentioned several times in the Quran, representing the axis of the world and universal man.

spiritual awakening

In Buddhist legend Queen Maya gave birth to Siddhartha Gautama, the Buddha-to-be, while standing and holding onto the branch of an overhanging sal tree. While still a *bodhisattva*, the young prince sat beneath a pipal tree at Bodh Gaya and vowed to wait in meditation until he had attained enlightenment, which he duly did. This tree, an old sacred fig tree (*Ficus religiosa*), is still known as "the Bodhi tree" and its direct descendant at Bodh Gaya (near Patna in modern-day Bihar province, India) is venerated by Buddhists to this day. Many Buddhist temples have a fig tree in their precincts, and the outlines of its heart-shaped leaves are sometimes painted on temple walls. The stone head of the Buddha seen here (left), at the ruins of a temple in Ayutthaya, central Thailand, has been enveloped by the roots of large banyan fig trees. Buddhist temple ruins (following pages) of Banteay Kdei at Angkor, Cambodia, have also been invaded by the gigantic roots of fig trees.

cottonwood tree

Each year, at the height of summer, the Native Americans of the Great Plains region of North America celebrate the Sun Dance. According to Lakota tradition, people offer as a sacrifice a four-day dance around a pole made from a particular type of poplar called a "cottonwood tree" (left). The tree is carefully chosen – it must be robust and approximately 10m (30ft) in height, with two of its branches forming a wide fork, like arms held up to the sky. The ceremony begins with a young girl striking the tree with a hatchet, whereupon about 10l (2gal) of crude sap runs out of the trunk. This sap is carefully collected, for it is considered to have healing powers. When the tree is cut down, men hold it so that the branches do not touch the ground; then the branches are removed and its leaves stripped so that only those on the crown remain. After this the cottonwood is planted in the centre of the dancing area, into a hole filled with food. Decked out with coloured ribbons and small bags of tobacco, it becomes the tree of life and the pivot of this collective ritual.

once upon a time...

///

n order to make the power of trees and forests accessible to the imagination, humans have filled them with beings similar to themselves, yet magical and different. As soon as towns and villages developed, the dense, forbidding woods became a place of refuge for outlaws, from highwaymen-bandits to noble and misunderstood idealists. Elves, fairies, ogres, witches, giants and gnomes have all been fellow forest inhabitants in stories and legends all over the world – sometimes menacing, sometimes helpful and good-natured, they enabled very ancient myths and morality tales, expressing our deepest fears and hidden hopes, to be acted out against the enigmatic backdrop of the forest.

"FOREST! IT IS YOUR SHADE AND MYSTERY,
YOUR AUGUST AND SOLITARY BRANCHES
WHOSE PROTECTION I WISH FOR IN MY LONELY SEPULCHRE,
IN YOUR SHADE I WISH TO SLEEP WHEN I DIE."
VICTOR HUGO, *LES CONTEMPLATIONS* (1856)

///
Just as the hazel stick of a water diviner leads him toward hidden water, black branches silhouetted in the moonlit night sky are like paths giving access to the land of dreams.

terrifying trees

In the literary masterpieces of Hindu spirituality known as the *Upanishad*s there is a description of the eternal cosmic tree Asvattha with its roots pointing heavenward into the sky, and its branches growing downward, thriving in this world, into the ground.

One member of the fig family, the Indian banyan or *Ficus benghalensis* (left), engages in an unusual means of reproduction and growth that is reminiscent of this account. Its seeds germinate on host trees (generally passed out by birds), growing epiphytically (in the open air) and sending aerial roots toward the ground. When the roots reach the earth they weld themselves to it and encircle the original tree trunk so tightly that they suffocate it. Once the wood of the carrier tree has decayed, all trace of it will have disappeared apart from the telltale evidence of large holes in the centre of the strangling fig tree.

last survivors
The Madagascar baobab, known in Malagasy as *renala* or "mother of the forest", is a strange-looking tree – its smooth, phallic trunk can reach about 25m (80ft) in height and up to 10m (33ft) in diameter, but it has tiny leaves that are extremely sparse. A remnant of the island's once dense forest, the "Avenue of the Baobabs" at Morondava (above) has survived because of the reluctance of local people to fell these giants, many of which are more than 800 years old. Myths explain that the

trees were turned upside down, so that their roots clung to the sky and their branches were buried in the earth, by a god, devil or supernatural hyena angered by having been among the last to arrive when the Earth was first filled with living things. The bulging trunk is a mechanism to cope with drought – the swollen trunk may hold as much as 100,000l (22,000gal) of water. The spongy trunk has a thin bark, which thirsty elephants sometimes pierce with their tusks to gain access to a life-saving drink.

spirit of the weeping willow
Native to northern China, Peking or Babylon willow (*Salix babylonica*) has been cultivated for millennia and exported to as far away as Europe. A Japanese legend recounts that long ago a man accepted a weeping willow from a neighbour who wanted to get rid of it because he suspected it was the source of all his misfortunes. Having replanted it in his garden, the man was surprised when, the next day, he found a ravishing young woman plaiting the hanging

branches as if they were her own hair. He married her and the couple had a child whom they called Yanagi, which means "willow". But one day the tree was cut down to repair a temple. The wife, who was none other than the willow's soul, died instantly and the tree, even though it had been felled, resisted all attempts to move it – that is until the child, speaking to it softly, seized a branch and slid it gently to where its wood was wanted. Gardens of weeping willows adorn the Magpie Bridge in Beijing's Changpu River Park (above).

enchanted forests

Fairytales are a channel for the primitive element that remains in all of us, appealing across the generations and containing all the ingredients needed for acting out gruesome terrors or delirious delights, improbable encounters or happy endings, in which the hero or heroine is irrevocably changed. The semi-darkness, the filtered light, the trees swaying in the wind, the mysterious crackling sounds underfoot, the sudden appearance of animals – all these and more are waiting for those, such as Snow White and Little Red Riding Hood, who dare to venture within the wooded setting. Danger lurks in the fairytale forest, where there live strange, legendary creatures with amazing powers, presenting fearsome obstacles to be overcome. Written by adults for children, fairytales are full of nostalgia for the magical world of the infant imagination, where any situation can be reversed. The forest is where the real interacts with the unreal.

in the great north

Yggdrasil, the enormous ash of Scandinavian mythology, is the axis of the universe, the World Tree, which links the three levels of the Viking cosmos: the upper world of the gods and light elves in Asgard; the middle worlds of humankind, dwarves and dark elves in Midgard, and of giants in the mountainous Jotunheim; and, finally, the lower world of the dead in Niflheim. Yggdrasil has an immense crown, abundant branches and is considered the guardian of the whole world. Its roots in Niflheim are continually gnawed by the monstrous serpent Nidhogg – and in this way the tree knows the sufferings of the universe. Yggdrasil translates as "the horse of Odin". It was after the god Odin had voluntarily endured the terrible ordeal of hanging for nine days and nights from Yggdrasil's branches that he had revealed to him the hidden meaning of the runes and acquired the mastery of writing and occult wisdom. Ash trees can become exceptionally stout – this example, at Clapton Court, Somerset (left), is the largest (girth 8.8m/28ft 10in) in England and may be more than 500 years old.

trees as symbols

///

Trees present us with an easily observable model of organization as well as of the dynamics of life and action, from the single to the multiple and vice versa. The tree's rootlets meet and gradually merge, becoming larger and larger roots, until they form a single trunk whose length no longer changes once the tree is adult, but whose diameter increases from year to year. In its upper part, the trunk divides into larger and smaller branches bearing leaves, flowers and fruit, in an abundance matched by that of the root system. The tree has positive associations of solidity, longevity and continuity; it gathers together into a single organism seemingly incongruous aspects, such as density and weightlessness, darkness and light – and it produces the ephemeral as well as the durable. For the humanists of the Renaissance, the tree was an allegory of learning; and in the modern era it has become a vehicle of information, a theoretical or graphic framework that permits us an overall view as well as providing us with the means to navigate from branch to branch. From genealogical charts to tree-structured computer files and decision trees, these giants of nature serve to plot the past or plan the future.

///

This beech tree in the wooded landscape of southern France's Basque Country has had its trunk cut over and over again at the same height and has ended up with a strange shape as a result. Among the Basque people a tree (albeit an oak rather than a beech) is the traditional symbol of their freedoms.

TREES THAT ARE PLANTED TO MARK THE BIRTH OF A CHILD CELEBRATE GROWTH AND LIFE; THOSE PLANTED ON TOMBS, IN MEMORY OF THE DEPARTED, REMIND US THAT EVERYTHING RETURNS TO THE EARTH AND BECOMES A SOURCE OF NEW LIFE.

social harmony

With its connections to both the earth and the sky, the tree provides an appropriate setting for the resolution of conflicts and the making of fair decisions. In Africa villagers have traditionally debated problems and community projects by gathering under a tree to "palaver" and thrash out discussion of the issue – a custom that the modernization of life has not put an end to, though today these "parliaments" are used for educational purposes, such as enabling doctors to explain the usefulness of a medicine and the people to ask questions and express reservations.

The importance of trees in the identity of some countries has led to the incorporation of tree symbols into various national flags, including the red maple leaf for Canada, the kapok tree for Equatorial Guinea and the cedar (left) for Lebanon.

tradition and modernity

A few days after the winter solstice, Christmas festivities celebrate the birth of Jesus, and in homes throughout the world the ancient custom of decorating a Christmas tree is practised. In Western Christianity the Nativity is celebrated liturgically as Christmastide on 25 December. Before Christianity there had been many pagan midwinter festivals, including one where Celtic Druids paid homage to an evergreen tree on 24 December. In the eighth century Saint Boniface went among the Germanic peoples as a missionary. Legend has it that he chopped down an oak tree that he found being worshipped at the winter solstice. When a fir tree grew in place of the felled oak the pagans were won round and he was able to recommend that a new fir "tree of the Child Jesus" be "planted" at Christmastide. The tradition continues in our own day, using varieties of conifer selected for the resistance of their needles. For example, the Douglas fir, seen here in Olympic National Forest, Washington State, USA, is one of the most popular types of Christmas tree.

families

Genealogy features prominently in many mythological and religious traditions. For example, the biblical Tree of Jesse describes the descent of Jesus through the line of David, king of Israel. Later, lineage was used to legitimize the continuity of temporal power by kings and emperors, who would claim the right to rule as descendants of an illustrious ancestor. In the traditional family tree, the common ancestor is the trunk, which is subdivided into as many branches as there are children, and these branches subdivide with each generation – the tree is then said to be "descendant". But if you wish to "trace your roots" and discover your ancestors the picture is reversed: you put yourself at the base and go back in time through your parents, then their parents, and so on; you add siblings to make the foliage denser, and develop your "ascendant" tree according to a geometrical progression which will be limited only by memory and the availability of archives. The structure of a family tree is evoked particularly strongly by this fan-trained pear tree (left) at Holkham Hall, Norfolk, England.

the human tree

The tree is used to provide an organizational framework to explain many things, from the inner workings of the human body to the classification of life on Earth. The *sefirot* of the Kabbalah, an ancient Jewish mystical tradition, represents as a "tree of life" the pathways that connect the emanations of the manifested universe. This system, connecting spirit and matter, is similar to the Indian system of *chakras*, which connects the structure of the human body with the cosmic energy of the universe. More tangible is the human body's bronchial tree – its method of respiration, revealed through dissection, which groups together all air circulation, from the inspiration of breath and the windpipe to the alveoli of the lungs; and then the reverse route, when the air has transmitted oxygen to the blood and taken in carbon dioxide, until the expiration of breath. (This silhouetted acacia in Namibia, left, mimics a lung.) At a microscopic level within the body the name dendrite refers to the branched extensions of nerve cells, and it comes from the Greek *dendron*, meaning "tree".

GLOSSARY

agroforestry A form of sustainable forest management in which harvesting of trees alternates with, or is mixed with, farming.

angiosperm Plant whose fertilized seeds are enclosed in a fruit, unlike gymnosperms where the seed is exposed.

arboretum Specialized botanic garden consisting of trees which may be a "forest" development, a "collection", a "themed" area or a "landscaped" area.

arboriculture The cultivation of fruit trees as distinguished from sylviculture.

bough Small branch

broad-leaved Tree belonging to the category of angiosperms.

bud Over-wintering structure from which branches, leaves, fruits and flowers grow.

budbreak Period during which a tree's buds open, letting the stems, flowers and fruits appear.

catkin A tassel or bunch of small flowers.

cellulose Fibre found mainly in wood, which is an important raw material in the manufacture of pulp for paper.

chlorophyll Green pigment contained in leaves, which is involved in the process of photosynthesis.

clump Young shoots appearing at the base of the trunk, after the tree has been cut or mutilated.

collar Lower circular area where the trunk joins the roots.

cone Fruit present in conifers where it takes two forms: male and female. The male cone provides the pollen which, once released, fertilizes the female cone.

conifer Tree belonging to the group of gymnosperms. Many of them have needles but some, like the ginkgo or larch, have other kinds of foliage.

cotyledon Seed leaf in the fruit of all angiosperm trees.

crown Upper part of the tree.

deciduous Describes a tree whose foliage falls in autumn, after a period of discoloration.

dendrochronology The dating of timber by counting the tree rings.

dicotyledon Flowering plant (angiosperm) that has two cotyledons (examples: hardwood plants and trees, annual or perennial plants).

dissemination Dispersal of seeds by wind, water, animals or by the plant itself.

ecosystem All the various living organisms that share the same space and interact with each other and their environment.

epiphyte Plant which grows on another tree and captures the moisture in the air without taking root in the earth (example: the banyan).

evapotranspiration Phenomenon that involves direct evaporation from the ground but also the loss of moisture from the foliage of trees and plants.

FAO Acronym for Food and Agriculture Organization, a United Nations organization for food and agriculture created in 1945 in Quebec.

follicle Dried fruit made up of a single carpel which splits on one side to let the seeds escape.

grass Monocotyledonous plant, usually perennial and with long leaves and inflorescence.

greenhouse effect Heating of the atmosphere due to the presence of "greenhouse" gases.

gymnosperm Plant with seeds not in a fruit but most often nestling in cones.

humus The upper layer of soil formed by the decomposition of organic matter.

inflorescence A grouping of flowers.

layer A new individual with a potential identical to that of the original tree, produced when the lower branches of certain trees touch the ground and put out roots.

leafing Phenomenon that occurs at the moment when a tree's leaves begin to grow.

leaflet A subdivision of the blade in a compound leaf.

ligature Constriction that impedes a tree's normal growth, often used when growing bonsais.

lignin One of the main components of wood, together with cellulose and hemicellulose.

Liliaceae Plant family with corms or rhizomes (example: tulips or lily-of-the-valley).

monocotyledon Angiosperm plant producing seeds that have only one cotyledon.

peduncle Stalk of a fruit or flower.

persistent Describes the foliage of a plant that remains green throughout the year. Conifers are generally persistent (except for the ginkgo and larches).

petiole Part of the leaf that connects the blade to the branch.

pharmacopoeia Catalogue of all medicines.

phloem Tubes through which sugar sap circulates from the leaves, where it has been made, to the whole of the tree.

photosynthesis Process by which plants trap light energy and carbon dioxide from the atmosphere and water from the soil to produce glucose.

phytotherapy Natural medicine based on specific plant use.

pistil Female organ including the ovary, the style and the stigma.

pollen Male fertilizing grains which form in the anther, the terminal part of the stamen.

pollination Release of pollen grains by the stamens and their deposition on the stigma.

Pollen tubes growing from the grains through the style to the ovary fertilize the ovules. These are then transformed into seeds.

resin A liquid, antiseptic and healing substance contained in the tree.

rib Vein in the leaf through which the sap circulates.

ring A year's growth of wood in the tree trunk, which enables its age to be calculated.

rootlet Ramification from the main root.

sap A liquid of water and minerals taken up from the ground and circulating in the trunk to reach the branches.

sapwood The part of the tree that is just beneath the bark, through which the sap circulates.

shrub Woody plant with many stems, unlike a tree which has a single trunk, usually reaching no more than 6–7m (20–23ft).

spore A single-cell structure for reproduction in plants that do not produce flowers and seeds.

stamen The flower's male organ.

stigma The female part of the flower situated at the end of the pistil, which receives the pollen.

stipe The trunk of monocotyledons which develops by accumulating successive phases of growth.

stump The part of the tree situated at ground and root level.

style Female part of the flower connecting the ovary with the stigma.

sucker Plant or stem which opens out from a bud on a root and benefits from the tree's food.

sylviculture Systematic exploitation of the forest heritage dating from the late nineteenth century.

twig Finest branch of a bough.

variety Type of tree which is of interest to sylviculture.

veteran tree A tree which, due to its great age, is part of the historic or cultural heritage.

xylem Canals that conduct water and minerals from the roots to the whole of the tree.

INDEX

PICTURE CREDITS

Pages 4–5 ©iStockphoto; **10–11** ©Eric Baccega/Photolibrary.com; **14** ©Ariadne Van Zandbergen/Photolibrary.com; **16–17** ©Robin Smith/Photolibrary.com; **18–19** ©Thinkstock LLC/Jupiterimages; **20–21** ©Martin Rugner/Photolibrary.com; **22tl** ©Photos.com/Jupiterimages; **22tr** ©Ablestock/Jupiterimages; **22bl** ©Rob Blakers/Photolibrary.com; **22br** ©Mark Bolton/Photolibrary.com; **23** ©John Glover/Photolibrary.com; **24–25** ©Carol Sharp/Photolibrary.com; **28** ©Clive Nichols/Photolibrary.com; **30–31** ©Comstock Images/Jupiterimages; **32–33** ©Eduardo Ripoll/Photolibrary.com; **34–35** ©David Muench/Corbis; **36–37** ©Ron Watts/Photolibrary.com; **38–39** ©Greg Vaughn/Photolibrary.com; **40** ©Loren McIntyre/Photolibrary.com; **42–43** ©Ulf Sjostedt/Photolibrary.com; **46** ©Bill Ross/Photolibrary.com; **48–49** ©Radius Images/Photolibrary.com; **50–51** ©Radius Images/Photolibrary.com; **52–53** ©FSG FSG/Photolibrary.com; **54–55** ©Brian K Miller/Photolibrary.com; **56** ©Clint Farlinger/Photolibrary.com; **58–59** ©Erich Kuchling/Photolibrary.com; **60–61** ©Agnès Duret/BiosPhoto; **62–63** ©Nick Norman/Photolibrary.com; **64–65** ©Kenichi Minoruda/Photolibrary.com; **66** ©Mike Slater/Photolibrary.com; **68–69** ©Photos.com/Jupiterimages; **70–71** ©Kevin Schafer/Photolibrary.com; **72–73** ©iStockphoto; **74–75** ©Rosseforp/Photolibrary.com; **78** ©Baldassini TIPS RF/Photolibrary.com; **80–81** ©IFA-BILDERTEAM GMBH/Photolibrary.com; **82** ©Corbis/Photolibrary.com; **84–85** ©Erich Kuchling/Photolibrary.com; **86–87** ©Liquid Library/Jupiterimages; **88–89** ©Raymond Forbes/Photolibrary.com; **90** ©Bildagentur RM/Photolibrary.com; **92–93** ©Anup Shah/Photolibrary.com; **94–95** ©Mary Plage/Photolibrary.com; **96** ©Michel Poinsignon & David Hackel/BiosPhoto; **97** ©Kerstin Hinze/BiosPhoto; **98–99** ©X.Richer–J.Bravo/Photolibrary.com; **100–101** ©Martin Harvey/Corbis; **102–103** ©Motor-Presse Syndication/Photolibrary.com; **104–105** ©Bill Ross/Photolibrary.com; **108** ©Guido Alberto Rossi/Photolibrary.com; **110–111** ©Ingram Publishing/Photolibrary.com; **112–113** ©Jacques Langevin/Corbis; **114–115** ©Johnny Stockshooter/Photolibrary.com; **116–117** ©Kathy Coatney/AgStock Images/Corbis; **118–119** ©Philip Wallick/Photolibrary.com; **120–121** ©Carol and Mike Werner/Photolibrary.com; **122–123** ©Roine Magnusson/Photolibrary.com; **124** ©Valentin Rodriguez/Photolibrary.com; **125** ©Nigel J.H. Smith/Photolibrary.com; **126** ©Josh McCulloch/Photolibrary.com; **128** ©Hervé Bruhat/Rapho/Eyedea; **130–131** ©Jeremy Woodhouse/Photolibrary.com; **132–133** ©Jacobs Jacobs/Photolibrary.com; **134–135** ©Michel Seitboun; **136–137** ©David Lorenz Winston/Photolibrary.com; **138–139** ©Chromorange RM/Photolibrary.com; **140** ©Photolibrary.com; **142–143** ©NASA/Corbis; **144–145** ©Remi Benali/Photolibrary.com; **146** ©Corbis/Photolibrary.com; **148–149** ©Harald Sund/Getty Images; **150–151** ©Bruno De Faveri/Photolibrary.com; **154** ©Fancy/Photolibrary.com; **156–157** ©Christina Krutz/Photolibrary.com; **158–159** ©Wallace Garrison/Photolibrary.com; **160–161** ©Niall Benvie/Photolibrary.com; **162–163** ©Michele Falzone/Photolibrary.com; **164–165** ©Martin Engelmann/Photolibrary.com; **166–167** ©Ron Crabtree/Photolibrary.com; **168** ©Keith Levit Photography/Photolibrary.com; **170–171** ©TED MEAD/Photolibrary.com; **172–173** ©Ariadne Van Zandbergen/Photolibrary.com; **174–175** ©Luis Castaneda Inc./Getty Images; **176–177** ©DesignPics Inc./Photolibrary.com; **178–179** ©Mark Bolton/Photolibrary.com; **180** ©Juan Carlos Cantero/Photolibrary.com; **182–183** ©Ursula Gahwiler/Photolibrary.com; **184–185** ©Greg Vaughn/Photolibrary.com; **186–187** ©Howard Rice/Photolibrary.com; **188–189** ©Juan-Carlos Muñoz/BiosPhoto.